DEPOSITIONS ANSWER BOOK

2019 Edition

PLI PRESS

PLI'S COMPLETE LIBRARY OF TREATISE TITLES

ART LAW

Art Law: The Guide for Collectors, Investors, Dealers & Artists

BANKING & COMMERCIAL LAW

Asset-Based Lending: A Practical Guide to Secured Financing
Consumer Financial Services Answer Book
Equipment Leasing–Leveraged Leasing
Financial Institutions Answer Book: Law, Governance, Compliance
Hillman on Commercial Loan Documentation
Hillman on Documenting Secured Transactions: Effective Drafting and Litigation
Maritime Law Answer Book

BANKRUPTCY LAW

Bankruptcy Deskbook
Personal Bankruptcy Answer Book

BUSINESS, CORPORATE & SECURITIES LAW

Accountants' Liability
Anti-Money Laundering: A Practical Guide to Law and Compliance
Antitrust Law Answer Book
Broker-Dealer Regulation
Conducting Due Diligence in a Securities Offering
Corporate Compliance Answer Book
Corporate Legal Departments: Practicing Law in a Corporation
Corporate Political Activities Deskbook
Corporate Whistleblowing in the Sarbanes-Oxley/Dodd-Frank Era
Covered Bonds Handbook
Cybersecurity: A Practical Guide to the Law of Cyber Risk
Derivatives Deskbook: Close-Out Netting, Risk Mitigation, Litigation
Deskbook on Internal Investigations, Corporate Compliance, and White Collar Issues
Directors' and Officers' Liability: Current Law, Recent Developments, Emerging Issues
Doing Business Under the Foreign Corrupt Practices Act
EPA Compliance and Enforcement Answer Book
Exempt and Hybrid Securities Offerings
Fashion Law and Business: Brands & Retailers
Financial Product Fundamentals: Law, Business, Compliance
Financial Services Mediation Answer Book
Financial Services Regulation Deskbook
Financially Distressed Companies Answer Book
Global Business Fraud and the Law: Preventing and Remedying Fraud and Corruption
Hedge Fund Regulation
Initial Public Offerings: A Practical Guide to Going Public
Insider Trading Law and Compliance Answer Book
Insurance and Investment Management M&A Deskbook
International Corporate Practice: A Practitioner's Guide to Global Success
Investment Adviser Regulation: A Step-by-Step Guide to Compliance and the Law
Legal Guide to the Business of Marijuana
Life at the Center: Reflections on Fifty Years of Securities Regulation
Mergers, Acquisitions and Tender Offers: Law and Strategies
Mutual Funds and Exchange Traded Funds Regulation
Outsourcing: A Practical Guide to Law and Business
Privacy Law Answer Book
Private Equity Funds: Formation and Operation
Proskauer on Privacy: A Guide to Privacy and Data Security Law in the Information Age
Public Company Deskbook: Complying with Federal Governance & Disclosure Requirements
SEC Compliance and Enforcement Answer Book
Securities Investigations: Internal, Civil and Criminal

Securities Law and Practice Deskbook
The Securities Law of Public Finance
Securities Litigation: A Practitioner's Guide
Social Media and the Law
Soderquist on Corporate Law and Practice
Sovereign Wealth Funds: A Legal, Tax and Economic Perspective
A Starter Guide to Doing Business in the United States
Technology Transactions: A Practical Guide to Drafting and Negotiating Commercial Agreements
Variable Annuities and Variable Life Insurance Regulation

COMMUNICATIONS LAW

Advertising and Commercial Speech: A First Amendment Guide
Sack on Defamation: Libel, Slander, and Related Problems
Telecommunications Law Answer Book

EMPLOYMENT LAW

Employment Law Yearbook
ERISA Benefits Litigation Answer Book
Labor Management Law Answer Book

ESTATE PLANNING AND ELDER LAW

Blattmachr on Income Taxation of Estates and Trusts
Estate Planning & Chapter 14: Understanding the Special Valuation Rules
International Tax & Estate Planning: A Practical Guide for Multinational Investors
Manning on Estate Planning
New York Elder Law
Stocker on Drawing Wills and Trusts

HEALTH LAW

FDA Deskbook: A Compliance and Enforcement Guide
Health Care Litigation and Risk Management Answer Book
Health Care Mergers and Acquisitions Answer Book
Medical Devices Law and Regulation Answer Book
Pharmaceutical Compliance and Enforcement Answer Book

IMMIGRATION LAW

Fragomen on Immigration Fundamentals: A Guide to Law and Practice

INSURANCE LAW

Business Liability Insurance Answer Book
Insurance Regulation Answer Book
Reinsurance Law

INTELLECTUAL PROPERTY LAW

Copyright Law: A Practitioner's Guide
Faber on Mechanics of Patent Claim Drafting
Federal Circuit Yearbook: Patent Law Developments in the Federal Circuit
How to Write a Patent Application
Intellectual Property Law Answer Book
Kane on Trademark Law: A Practitioner's Guide
Likelihood of Confusion in Trademark Law
Patent Claim Construction and *Markman* Hearings
Patent Law: A Practitioner's Guide
Patent Licensing and Selling: Strategy, Negotiation, Forms
Patent Litigation
Pharmaceutical and Biotech Patent Law
Post-Grant Proceedings Before the Patent Trial and Appeal Board
Substantial Similarity in Copyright Law
Trade Secrets: A Practitioner's Guide

LITIGATION

Arbitrating Commercial Disputes in the United States
Class Actions and Mass Torts Answer Book
Depositions Answer Book
Electronic Discovery Deskbook
Essential Trial Evidence: Brought to Life by Famous Trials, Films, and Fiction
Expert Witness Answer Book
Evidence in Negligence Cases
Federal Bail and Detention Handbook
How to Handle an Appeal
Medical Malpractice: Discovery and Trial
Product Liability Litigation: Current Law, Strategies and Best Practices
Sinclair on Federal Civil Practice
Trial Handbook

REAL ESTATE LAW

Commercial Ground Leases
Friedman on Contracts and Conveyances of Real Property
Friedman on Leases
Holtzschue on Real Estate Contracts and Closings: A Step-by-Step Guide to Buying and Selling Real Estate
Net Leases and Sale-Leasebacks

TAX LAW

The Circular 230 Deskbook: Related Penalties, Reportable Transactions, Working Forms
The Corporate Tax Practice Series: Strategies for Acquisitions, Dispositions, Spin-Offs, Joint Ventures, Financings, Reorganizations & Restructurings
Foreign Account Tax Compliance Act Answer Book
Internal Revenue Service Practice and Procedure Deskbook
International Tax & Estate Planning: A Practical Guide for Multinational Investors
International Tax Controversies: A Practical Guide
International Trade Law Answer Book: U.S. Customs Laws and Regulations
Langer on Practical International Tax Planning
The Partnership Tax Practice Series: Planning for Domestic and Foreign Partnerships, LLCs, Joint Ventures & Other Strategic Alliances
Private Clients Legal & Tax Planning Answer Book
Transfer Pricing Answer Book

GENERAL PRACTICE PAPERBACKS

Anatomy of a Mediation: A Dealmaker's Distinctive Approach to Resolving Dollar Disputes and Other Commercial Conflicts
Attorney-Client Privilege Answer Book
Drafting for Corporate Finance: Concepts, Deals, and Documents
Pro Bono Service by In-House Counsel: Strategies and Perspectives
Smart Negotiating: How to Make Good Deals in the Real World
Thinking Like a Writer: A Lawyer's Guide to Effective Writing & Editing
Working with Contracts: What Law School Doesn't Teach You

DEPOSITIONS
ANSWER BOOK
2019 Edition

Thomas R. Jackson

Practising Law Institute
New York City

#241251

QUESTIONS ABOUT THIS BOOK?

If you have questions about billing or shipments, or would like information on our other products, please contact our **customer service department** at info@pli.edu or at (800) 260-4PLI.

For any other questions or suggestions about this book, contact PLI's **editorial department** at: plipress@pli.edu.

For general information about Practising Law Institute, please visit **www.pli.edu.**

Legal Editor: Lori Wood

LCCN: 2018938581
ISBN: 978-1-4024-3121-0

About the Author

TOM JACKSON graduated from Western Kentucky University, *summa cum laude,* in 1976 with a Bachelor of Arts degree in economics and government. Tom went on to law school at Duke University, graduating in 1979, *Order of the Coif,* and immediately started working at Jones Day. Tom's practice focused on a variety of litigation-related matters, primarily in the areas of antitrust, intellectual property, and securities litigation. He retired from Jones Day at the end of 2016.

Early in his career at Jones Day, Tom took an interest in ensuring that younger lawyers had an opportunity to learn about litigation skills prior to putting them to use in the real world. Tom helped develop Jones Day's litigation skills training program, which includes a program on depositions. Tom has taught, and continues to teach, the Jones Day training programs. In addition, Tom has taught at the National Institute of Trial Advocacy's National Trial Program, at its Pittsburgh Trial Program, and at Emory Law School's Kessler-Edison Trial Practice Program. Since retiring, Tom has also taught a class at SMU Law School on depositions.

Tom takes lawyer training seriously, and he hopes that his book will assist other young lawyers about to embark on the deposition process.

Table of Chapters

Table of Contents

Chapter 3 Preliminary Practical Matters

Chapter 4 Preparing to Take the Deposition

Chapter 5 The Deposition Day

Chapter 6 The Form of the Question Matters

Chapter 8 Expert Witness Depositions

Chapter 10 Preparing the Witness and Defending the Deposition

Acknowledgments

The views and comments expressed in this book are mine. All errors are my responsibility. That being said, there are many people who have contributed to my views about the deposition process. A special thanks to Joseph L. McEntee. Joe was the first person to permit me to take an actual deposition and was always helpful with suggestions and advice throughout my career.

I have also been blessed to have taught for a long time with two dear friends, Michael Ginsberg and Paul Zwier. Mike, a partner with Jones Day, and Paul, Professor of Law at Emory Law School, have influenced my view on all aspects of the litigation process, including depositions. I am sure they will see several views expressed in this book.

And a special shout out to Tori Bliss and Hector Velez for assistance with preparing the chart in Appendix A of state rules applicable to depositions. Tori and Hector are both currently clerking for federal judges, but without their efforts, the chart would never have seen the light of day.

I must also express my thanks to PLI for the opportunity to write this book. They have shown great patience and provided incredible support. Lori Wood has gone above and beyond in the role of my editor. Her insights and suggestions have been invaluable. If a mistake exists in the book, I failed to heed Lori's suggestion.

Finally, my family has been incredibly supportive throughout. Lots of questions about the status of the book kept me focused until I could finally announce the book's completion.

I hope you find the book helpful.

Tom Jackson

Introduction

An answer book requires questions to answer. The first question that comes to mind is why an answer book about depositions? Depositions are the key component of all litigation matters that survive a motion to dismiss. In depositions, parties discover the theories, legal and factual, of their opponent and they explore the validity of their own case theories and themes. Why does the opportunity for such theory exploration matter? Because what you learn in the deposition process guides your evolving case strategy—whether to settle and, if so, at what value, or proceed to trial. That knowledge also sets up potential additional motion practice, guides further discovery efforts, and underlies the overall case valuation.

Very few litigation matters that survive motions to dismiss are resolved by trials. Lawyers, judges, and professors have bemoaned the loss of the jury trial from American jurisprudence. Most litigation matters settle, are resolved by courts on additional motion practice, or dismissed voluntarily. Why is this possible?

Under the American system,[1] the parties to a civil lawsuit are allowed extensive pretrial discovery of each other. The deposition plays a key role in that discovery process. Sure, more time is spent collecting, reviewing, and producing documents, but the deposition allows those documents to be translated into case value. The questioning of witnesses allows that story to come to life and permits a party's story to be evaluated. From the evaluation, the story either becomes part of the summary judgment motion, or it becomes the baseline for gauging how a jury would receive and reward that story.

---

1. The criminal system does not allow similar pretrial discovery. The obligation is on the government to provide the defense with "exculpatory" materials uncovered in its investigation. Defense counsel conducts their own investigation, but the defense lacks the ability to compel pretrial testimony under oath.

Even though most cases settle or are resolved on motion, the litigator must approach each case as if this is the case that will go to trial. Failure to take that approach leads to poorly conducted depositions, which can lead to higher settlement costs or even a negative case outcome.

Knowing the ins and outs of the deposition process has become very important in today's litigation world. By the mastery of that deposition process, litigants become better equipped to handle their cases. Hence, an answer book on depositions.

This book seeks to answer the questions that arise at any stage of the deposition process. I hope the question-and-answer format will allow the reader to navigate quickly to areas of primary concern and will be a ready resource for both the novice and the expert.

We will start with the basics of a deposition, including how to schedule and arrange one, and proceed to the harder issues of how to prepare for, ask questions during, and defend one. The role of defense counsel has evolved dramatically over the years. And, we will explain that defending a deposition begins with preparing the witness for the deposition.

The second question that might come to mind is why is this author the right one to answer deposition questions? This is a good question. The author's first deposition, over thirty-five years ago, was not one to use as a model for the deposition process. With no prior training and only limited opportunity to observe others, the author felt his way through the process, making lots of mistakes, and learning the hard way. To help others avoid those pitfalls, the author has been teaching deposition-related courses for the last twenty-five years. The answers in this book are an amalgamation of both real-life experience and those years of teaching.

1

Purpose of a Deposition

A deposition permits a party to explore the facts held by an individual or an entity bearing on the case at hand. Depositions occur well before trial and allow the party taking the deposition to learn the facts held by the other side and third parties. Too often, depositions are used to confirm the facts already known to one side. Depositions, properly done, do so much more and provide an avenue for accurate case assessments, and when required, for trial.

This chapter provides an overview of the various purposes that depositions serve. For each deposition that an attorney plans to conduct, he or she must determine which purpose or purposes might apply, as that will govern the types of questions that will be asked, the approach the questioner will take, and the tone of the questions asked.

The Purposes of a Deposition

Q 1.1 What are the purposes of taking a deposition?

There are at least six reasons to take a deposition:

1. Seek discovery
2. Seek admissions
3. Test theories
4. Gain material for motions or trial
5. Preserve testimony
6. Observe witnesses for the other side.

You may well develop other reasons, but do not fall for the false premise that a deposition can only be taken for one purpose at a time. Depositions often seek to cover all of these stated purposes simultaneously. Part of the pre-deposition preparation process requires figuring out the purposes you wish to cover and deciding the order in which to address each one.

A Discovery Deposition

Q 1.2 How does a deposition seek discovery?

Discovery comprises three types of materials—documents, physical evidence, and testimony. The deposition deals with the testimonial aspect, but can also lead to other types of discovery material. The deposition may use documentary and physical evidence, but it does so in a way that has a witness explain, expound, and add color. The deposition may also identify gaps in the prior document or physical discovery. The attorney for one side cannot roam through the records of the opposition, but can ask questions to uncover how and where documents and other materials are stored, identify the custodians, and determine whether those locations have been searched for responsive materials.

Not all witnesses are candidates for assisting with discovery issues. Depending on the witness's relation to the case, a witness might know additional areas of discovery or be helpful in explaining the discovery already provided. And, since most depositions are now subject to a time limitation—for example, the Federal Rules of Civil Procedure provide a presumptive seven-hour limitation (see chapter 2)—the questioner must make careful allocation of the time spent seeking additional discovery. There are no hard and fast rules that govern the allocation of time to particular purposes. The questioner must be alert for missing gaps in the information provided and be prepared to explore those missing gaps as the opportunity arises. For example, you probably would not think to pursue discovery issues with the CEO of a company. But, if the discovery issue is key information that has yet to be provided, a particularly good question for the CEO is who would he/she ask for that information.

A Deposition Seeking Admissions

Q 1.3 How does a deposition seek admissions?

By framing the questions correctly, a skilled questioner can eliminate issues from the case. The secret is learning how to phrase the question (essentially to make it short, without qualifiers, and limited to a single fact; see discussion in chapter 6), listen carefully to the answer, and then rephrase the question to remove any words that prevented the witness from answering the question with an unqualified yes. Since most witnesses are skeptical of deposition questions and look for ways to qualify their answers, the questioner must be prepared to spend the time required to make each admission-seeking question very simple and clear.

Admissions are the cornerstones of building your case. Each key fact admitted by the other side leaves one less matter you must prove in order to prevail. And, because it comes from the mouths of the other side, the fact finder will give the admission greater weight. With admissions, you build your case theory. Sometimes, the building process requires you to tear down your theory and start anew. This process permits a strong case theory to arise eventually—one with which the fact finder can easily agree.

Admissions also support motion practice. The best summary judgment motions are those that are based on concessions from the other side that support your legal theory. But, most witnesses will not admit so readily that their case lacks legal merit or that they are skewing the events to bolster their side, building on those small admissions until they show that result. The deposition skill becomes asking for small concessions that show that result.

A Deposition Testing Theories

Q 1.4 How does a deposition test theories?

Lawyers are constantly thinking of ways to explain to others why their side should prevail. In doing so, they hypothesize about the motives and rationale behind the decisions made by the other side. A defense lawyer might speculate that the plaintiff's injuries are not related to use of the client's product. The plaintiff's lawyer might imagine that the defendant manufacturer ignored safety concerns to maximize profits. These lawyers might be right, but what if they are wrong?

Imagine the impact at trial if the other side explains their actions in such a way that defeats any theory of liability. Our hypothetical lawyer is devastated and the client's case ends. Could this result have been avoided? Perhaps, through deposition questions, our hypothetical lawyer could have learned of the explanation before trial. That explanation might confirm the original hypothesis. If not, the lawyer still has time to develop a new theory or to revise the existing one to account for the explanation. The lawyer also has time to use additional discovery to determine the strength of the explanation.

Some lawyers believe that testing theories during the deposition provides the other side with insight into their case. These lawyers believe that they can anticipate and negate any explanations that might be offered later. What if they are wrong? That is the risk taken by not exploring your case theories and confirming that the evidence will allow that theory to prevail. Your client's case suffers. And, since so few cases go to trial, what is the real goal of keeping your theory from the other side? Odds are that the other side has a good feel for exactly the theory you will try to run anyway. It is equally likely that the other side will have tested its case theories during the depositions of your witnesses. You might also find that the settlement value rises as the other side hears your theories confirmed.

A Deposition Supporting Trial Motions

Q 1.5 How do depositions gain material for motions or trial?

In testing theories, the questioner should also seek specific factual concessions that support the questioner's side. Usually, there are an array of facts not disputed. Using the deposition process to identify the areas where there are no disputes goes a long way to establish support for a summary judgment motion. The motion can be tailored to address only the areas in dispute. And, even if the summary judgment motion fails, knowing the areas of agreement will simplify the trial testimony and number of witnesses required to prove undisputed points.

To achieve this objective, you must have a handle on your client's view of events and on what the documents show. These alone are not enough. You must also have a keen understanding of the law applicable to the claims being asserted. With the law as a guide, the questioner begins deposition preparation by outlining the factual areas to address the legal elements of the claim. A negligence case will focus on the actions that led to the incident, the circumstances surrounding the parties at the time the incident occurred, and what could have been done to prevent the accident from happening. A contract case will focus on a contract, its relevant terms, and the events leading to the dispute over compliance with the terms of the contract.

As you think about the questions that will assist with proving your case theory, assume that the case will proceed to trial. Always ask yourself how the information you seek in the deposition will assist with the trial and, as importantly, how the evidence will play in the courtroom. Those concepts assist in framing the areas of questions you want to ask at the deposition and how the answers can be used in pretrial motions.

A Deposition Preserves Testimony

Q 1.6 How can a deposition be used to preserve testimony?

Sometimes there are concerns that the witness with important testimony about a key event will not be available for trial. In the best of cases, this unavailability arises because of a vacation around the world. In the worst of times, there is a fear that the witness will not live long enough for discovery to proceed to the discovery phase. What to do in either case?

The process will vary depending on the jurisdiction involved and whether or not a complaint has already been filed. If the underlying case has not yet been filed and the case is in federal court, Rule 27 of the Federal Rules of Civil Procedure lays out the process:

1. File a verified petition in the district where the expected deponent resides; and
2. The petition must request an order permitting the deposition and must show:
    a. That the petitioner expects to be a party to an action in a U.S. court but cannot presently sue or cause suit to be brought;
    b. The subject of the future action and the petitioner's interest;
    c. The facts that the petitioner seeks to establish by the deposition and the reason it must be perpetuated;[1]
    d. The identity of the expected adverse parties and their addresses; and
    e. The name and address of the proposed deponent and the expected substance of their testimony.

As you might expect, the anticipated adverse parties must receive notice of the request at least twenty-one days before the hearing. The court then "must" issue an order to perpetuate testimony if it finds that doing so "may prevent a failure or delay of justice." The court may allow the deposition only on written questions. But, if allowed, the deposition may be used just as any other deposition in a case already filed.

If the case is already filed, the question is whether the other side will agree that the deposition is needed to perpetuate testimony. If so, the normal deposition process addressed in more detail in chapter 5 should be followed. You might also need to request court permission if the time for deposition discovery has not yet arrived under the case management order. If the other side fails to agree, the process is similar to that used prior to an action being filed. You must file a contested motion with the court and convince the court of the need to proceed with the deposition prior to the normal discovery window.

A Deposition Permits Witness Evaluation

Q 1.7 How does a deposition allow a party to evaluate witnesses?

What a witness says is important. But, how a witness answers a question might be even more important. We have all met people who are not believable no matter what they say. We do not like their attitude or their appearance and conclude that they will not make a great witness no matter what they have to say. The other side will make the exact same judgments about your witnesses. The deposition allows you to observe the witness and make those judgment calls.

With the opportunity to observe comes the burden of asking enough "hard" questions to gauge realistically a witness's demeanor. What's a hard question? It is a question that goes to one of the key issues. A key question seeks to uncover the party's motive for behaving as they did, or to establish a disputed fact in your favor. The form of the question is not "hard." There is no need for shouting, a stern face, or any other melodrama. Sometimes, the best question is simply "why did you do that?"

As you listen to the answer, pay attention to the words used by the witness but pay more attention to the facial expressions and the body language. Those non-verbal signs are the ones that will guide your assessment of the witness. And, you can use those non-verbal signs to tell you areas of inquiry where you must follow up. Witnesses often give non-verbal cues in areas where they are uncomfortable testifying. The skillful questioner seeks to identify the cause of the discomfort.

Note to Chapter 1

1. The testimony sought to be perpetuated must be evidence that cannot come easily from other sources. *See In re* Deiulemar Compagnia Di Navigazione S.p.A., 198 F.3d 473 (4th Cir. 1999).

2

Rules Governing Depositions

Depositions are powerful tools for the skilled litigator. But, knowing the purposes for which a deposition may be used will not alone create a successful deposition experience. Depositions, like all forms of discovery, are governed by a set of rules. Those rules govern the timing, location, and manner of taking a deposition. Understanding those rules, and realizing they vary by jurisdiction, are what make the deposition tool powerful. Both the taking lawyer and the defending lawyer must understand how the rules impact their role in the deposition.

A deposition that does not comply with the rules does not lead to useful results. The testimony might be excluded and the offending lawyer might face sanctions.

The Source of the Rules Governing Depositions

Q 2.1 What rules govern taking a deposition?

The correct answer depends on whether the case is in federal or state court and may also depend on where the witness resides. A chart in Appendix A of this book contains basic information for each state and federal district court about the number of depositions allowed, the timing for when depositions may begin, the length of depositions, and any special rules for defending a deposition. This chapter, however, will focus on the Federal Rules of Civil Procedure. The rules pertaining to depositions are scattered throughout, for a reason apparently only known to the drafters of those rules.

The Federal Rules on Depositions

Q 2.2 How do the federal rules approach depositions?

Absent some unusual circumstance, no discovery takes place until after the court conducts a discovery conference, as laid out in Rule 26(f). Prior to that conference, the parties must confer about several matters:

1. the nature of the claims and defenses and the possibilities for quickly resolving the case;
2. the pretrial disclosures required by Rule 26(a)(1);
3. issues relating to preservation of evidence; and
4. a proposed discovery plan.

See Rule 26(f)(2). The discovery plan must also address several specific topics, including changes to the initial disclosures, the date when those disclosures will be made, the subjects where discovery is needed, whether discovery should occur in phases, any issues with preservation or form of electronic data production, the manner for dealing with claims of privilege, any changes to the limitations on discovery, and any other matter that the parties believe appropriate. Rule 26(f)(3).

Q 2.2.1 What are the limits imposed on depositions?

The rules impose default limitations on the number of depositions that may occur, the length of those depositions, and the time when depositions may begin. Some rules also impose obligations on the conduct of the defending attorney.

Q 2.2.2 What are the default limits on depositions in the federal rules?

Rule 26(d)(1) provides that neither party may seek discovery until after the parties have conferred before the Rule 26(f) conference. Cases exempt from the pretrial disclosure process under Rule 26(a)(1)(B)[1] may begin discovery earlier. The only exception to the delay in the start of depositions arises when a party seeks leave of court because the proposed "deponent is expected to leave the United States and be unavailable for examination in this country after that time." Rule 30(a)(2)(iii). And, even though not set out in the rule, a party can also seek leave of court to depose a witness earlier resulting from other grounds that create an emergency.

Rule 30(a)(2)(i) sets the presumptive limit on the number of depositions at ten for each party. Rule 30(d)(1) sets the time limit for the deposition to one day of seven hours. The court *must* allow additional time if "needed to fairly examine" the witness or if the seven-hour time limit was shortened by the conduct of the witness, his counsel, or a third party.

The deposition limitations were added in 2000 to avoid unnecessary expense in litigation. Prior to that time, the only way to limit either the number of depositions or their individual length was to petition the court for a protective order.

Q 2.3 Can the limits be changed?

Yes, but not without the court's approval. If you think your case will require over ten depositions, the topic should be raised early with the other side beginning with the Rule 26(f) conference. The resulting discussion often leads to an agreement on a new number of depositions. In some areas of the country, the practice is to focus on the total of hours that a party may spend on depositions. Instead of fifteen depositions, the parties might agree that each side can take up to 100 hours of depositions. Unless specifically altered by agreement, the individual limit of seven hours per day for one witness remains in place. And, the court may not agree with the parties' proposed adjustments to the default limits. Some courts prefer to enter a lower number of depositions or hours for depositions with an instruction that the parties return to seek more depositions if required. The parties know that they need a good reason to seek additional relief.

The Rules for the Defending Lawyer

Q 2.4 What rules apply to the defending lawyer?

The practical issues relating to defending a deposition are discussed in chapter 10. Rule 30(c)(2) notes that the defending lawyer may object to a deposition question but must do so "concisely in a nonargumentative and nonsuggestive manner." The rules seek to end the age old practice of lawyers using their objections as a way to assist the witness with answers.[2] The tactic of responding to every question with the advice to answer the question "if you know" or "if you remember" is no longer allowed. Called "speaking" objections, lawyers may no longer engage in such conduct.

Several jurisdictions permit the defending lawyer only to utter the phrase "object to the form of the question." The defending lawyer may say no more unless asked the basis of the objection. These jurisdictions believe this approach balances the defending lawyer's right to protect the record against the evils of a lawyer attempting to testify for the witness. Other jurisdictions allow the addition of a limited explanation of the objection. The defending lawyer might say, for example, "objection vague" or "objection compound" without running afoul of the rules.[3]

There are also several jurisdictions that impose specific limitations on the ability of counsel defending the deposition to consult with the witness about the substance of their testimony. Federal courts are split on the proper procedure. Some courts, keying off of Rule 30(c)(1)'s requirement that the examination "proceed as they would at trial," prohibit any discussions between the lawyer and the witness until all questions have been asked.[4] Other federal courts take a less strict view of the attorney conference and permit conferences if no question is pending at the time.[5] All courts make an exception for conversations where an issue of privilege arises whether a question is pending or not. Like all exceptions, the lawyer must be sure not to abuse this limited right.

Appendix A endeavors to capture those rules as they exist in state rules, but beware that local state courts may have their own specific views on the proper behavior of a defending lawyer. Also beware that some rules may be contained in case law, and may not be codified.

Notes to Chapter 2

1. These cases are exempt: cases for review of an administrative record; a forfeiture action in rem arising from a federal statute; a habeas corpus or other challenge to a criminal proceeding; an action brought by a person in custody; an action to quash an administrative summons or subpoena; an action by the United States to recover benefit payments; an action by the United States to collect a student loan guaranteed by the United States; an ancillary proceeding to a matter in another court; or an action to enforce an arbitration award. FED. R. CIV. P. 26(a)(1)(B).

2. One of the tenets of U.S.-style litigation is that the parties, through discovery, gain a mutual knowledge of all relevant facts. But that tenet is always in tension with individual desires to win the case by preventing the other side from learning all relevant facts. Whether it's games with document discovery or speaking objections designed to help a witness answer hard questions, by 1979, Justice Powell thought that courts needed to have the ability "to curb the widespread abuse of discovery that is a prime cause of delay and expense in civil litigation." ACF Indus., Inc. v. EEOC, 439 U.S. 1081, 1086 (1979).

3. These differences in approach require a careful review of the applicable rules prior to the first deposition.

4. The Eastern District of Pennsylvania decision in Hall v. Clifton Precision, 150 F.R.D. 525, 528 (E.D. Pa. 1993), is often credited as the leading decision limiting the right of contact during the deposition. Noting that "[t]he witness comes to testify, not to indulge in a parody of Charlie McCarthy, with lawyers coaching or bending the witness's words to mold to a legally convenient record," the court outlawed all such conferences and allowed the deposing lawyer to ask questions about what occurred during breaks.

5. The District of Nevada decision in *In re* Stratosphere, 182 F.R.D. 614, 621 (D. Nev. 1998), is most often cited for the more relaxed view of conferences among lawyers and witnesses during the deposition. Finding that the witness had a right to counsel, and absent any abuse, the court found "[w]e all want the witness's answers, but not at the sacrifice of his or her right to the assistance of counsel."

3

Preliminary Practical Matters

Before you can ask your first question, there is a lot of work to do. Depositions do not magically come to fruition. Arranging a deposition can take time. Thought must be given to who to depose given whatever limits on depositions have been imposed. Then, once witnesses have been identified, decisions must be made regarding who should be deposed first. And, arranging for the deposition requires working with court reporters, lawyers for the witness, and sometimes process servers. Bringing these preliminary matters together allows the deposition to occur.

The Process of Arranging the Deposition

Q 3.1 Now that I want to take a deposition, how do I make it happen?

Start by contacting the counsel for the witness, if he or she has one. If you don't know whether the witness is represented by counsel, that is the first question you should ask the witness, prior to the deposition.[1] Witnesses not represented, and even third parties who are represented, should be candidates for an informal interview as opposed to a formal deposition. The informal setting often provides a better chance to learn what the witness knows. And, following the interview you can decide whether that witness's knowledge is worth taking one of your limited depositions.

When the potential witness is not available for an interview or the interview leads to a decision to formalize the testimony, the deposition process must be engaged. First, ask the witness's counsel for available dates. Asking first avoids unnecessary time and expense of arranging a deposition only to learn that the witness or his or her lawyer is not available on the selected date. If the witness or counsel fails to provide dates, you can select dates arbitrarily to force the process along by serving a notice or a subpoena.

The Deposition Notice or Subpoena

Q 3.2 What is a notice or a subpoena?

Both are formal documents required to provide formal notice of your intent to take a deposition. A notice of a deposition is used for depositions of parties to the litigation and need only be served on counsel of record. The notice is issued by the attorney seeking to take the deposition. A subpoena is used for third parties and, though now also issued by the lawyer seeking the deposition,[2] carries the court's command to appear at the noticed time.

A notice or subpoena should always be issued for a deposition. Be wary of following an informal process of notifying the other side of your deposition plan. When something goes wrong and you need the court's assistance, the absence of a formal notice will be problematic because the lack of formality will be a basis to deny the relief you seek.

Q 3.2.1 What must a notice or a subpoena contain?

A deposition notice need not be overly complicated. You must give "reasonable written notice" to every other party. You must also set forth the name and address of the witness and the "time and place of the deposition." Rule 30(b)(1). Finally, the notice must state the method by which the testimony will be recorded.

A subpoena must state the court from which it is issued, the title and civil action number, command the identified person to "attend and testify," and set forth the text of Rule 45(d) (dealing with protective orders for the benefit of the person subject to a subpoena) and (e) (dealing with production of information requested by a subpoena). Rule 45(a).

Both the notice and the subpoena may also seek the production of documents or other tangible things. To do so, you provide a list of the documents requested. Rule 30(a)(2) and Rule 45(a)(1)(C)–(D). Just like normal document requests, your demand for documents must be relevant and "proportional to the needs of the case" with a notice. Rule 26(b)(1). For a subpoena, you are required "to take reasonable steps to avoid imposing undue burden or expense" on the non-party. Rule 45(d)(1).

Q 3.2.2 How do I serve a notice or a subpoena?

You serve a deposition notice as you would any other pleading in a case. A subpoena, which is used for depositions of those not in your case, may be served by anyone, not a party, who is over eighteen years old. The person named in the subpoena must be served.[3] And, you must tender to the witness during service a witness fee of $40 for one day plus round trip mileage to the place of the deposition.[4] Rule 45(b)(1). A subpoena may be served anywhere in the United States, but it may not command a person to travel more than "100 miles of where the person resides, is employed, or regularly transacts business" for the deposition. Rules 45(b)(2) and 45(c)(1)(A).[5]

Because there may be a later dispute about whether service of a subpoena was made, the best practice is to use a third-party process server who can testify to the fact of service if necessary. This adds expense to the process, but if the witness fails to show, you must have proof of service. The other parties attending the deposition would otherwise be entitled to "reasonable expense" for attending the deposition (which includes attorney fees). Rule 30(g).

Deposition of a Corporate Entity

Q 3.2.3 What if I need to depose an entity instead of an individual?

Sometimes it is impossible to identify specific individuals within an organization that possess the information you need for your side of the case. Occasionally, no single employee of an organization has all of the information you need. What do you do? The federal rules, and those of several states, permit taking the deposition of the entity. Rule 30(b)(6) allows the deponent to be "a public or private corporation, a partnership, an association, a governmental agency, or other entity."[6]

The full scope of the 30(b)(6) deposition will be discussed in chapter 7. For the present discussion, the important point is that the option to depose the entity is available to "avoid the bandying by corporations where individual . . . employees disclaim knowledge of facts clearly known to the corporation."[7] The entity may select its witnesses but the rule requires those witnesses be prepared on the topics listed in the 30(b)(6) notice.

The 30(b)(6) deposition provides one way to ease into the full discovery phase and a way to get information from a third-party entity quickly. You can use the 30(b)(6) deposition to identify the most important people for further discovery. You can also use it to ensure you have the relevant documents.

Requesting Documents As Part of the Deposition

Q 3.2.4 Speaking of documents, can you ask for documents as part of the deposition?

Yes. Rule 30(b)(2) allows for a document request to be part of the deposition notice or subpoena. For a third party, the request is called a subpoena duces tecum. In Latin, the phrase means "under penalty to bring with you." For parties, Rule 30(b)(2) provides that "a request under Rule 34 to produce documents" may be included.

These document requests are governed by Rule 26(b)(1). As recently amended, the document requests must be "proportional to the needs of the case." The rule lists several factors that the court should consider in making that decision: importance of requested discovery to the issues in the case; amount in controversy; relative access to the information; the relative resources of the parties; importance of the requested discovery to resolving the issue; and whether the burden outweighs the benefit. Gone is the concept that materials that "may lead to the discovery of admissible evidence" may be pursued. While the proportionality concept has been a part of the federal rules for some time,[8] the new rules seek to give greater consideration to that concept at the outset of discovery.

The Next Step After the Notice/Subpoena Has Been Served

Q 3.3 Now that the notice has been served, what's next?

Prior to issuing the notice, you will have decided upon a time and location for the deposition to take place since that information is in the notice. If you had not agreed on the time and place for the deposition in advance, do not be surprised if the lawyer for the witness calls to change the date and/or the location.[9] Most witnesses have a life other than waiting for your deposition notice. Absent exceptional circumstances, such as an approaching end of discovery deadline, the better practice is to accommodate a witness's reasonable requests. A reviewing court would expect such agreement. Issue a new notice or subpoena reflecting any changes agreed upon to the time and location of the deposition.[10]

With the time and the location now settled, the party noticing the deposition must provide a court reporter. We think of the court reporter as taking a stenographic record of the deposition. But, the means of recording need not be stenographic. Rule 30(b)(3) provides that the deposition may be recorded by audio, audiovisual, or stenographic means. That same rule also requires that the means of recording be contained in the notice.

Q 3.3.1 How do you select a court reporter?

The record generated by a court reporter is the most valuable part of the deposition. Only that record of the deposition may be used for any later purpose. Selecting the right court reporter is therefore important. While experience with the court reporter is the best indicator, there are often situations where that experience will lack. For depositions outside your normal area, the best resource may still be your local counsel or other lawyer you know in the area. Your local counsel has a vested interest in ensuring your continued satisfaction and will search to find a reputable reporter in another jurisdiction.

The parties may also agree to use the same court reporter, or court reporting firm, for the entire case. The advantages of selecting a common court reporter for all depositions include greater familiarity with the language unique to the case, ease of keeping up with sequential numbered exhibits (if you choose such an approach), and the opportunity for cost savings.

Some parties even agree to have the court reporter travel to the deposition location. In a case with many unique terms, the familiarity of the reporter with the case may outweigh the extra costs of travel. If you select this approach, make sure that the court reporter can swear in the witness in the location of the deposition. A deposition may be taken before "an officer authorized to administer oaths either by federal law or by the law of the place of examination."[11] FED. R. CIV. P. 28(a)(1)(A). An "officer" means a person appointed by the court or designated by the parties under Rule 29(a).[12]

If the deposition is to be taken outside of the United States, Rule 28(b) allows the deposition to be taken under any treaty or convention, under a letter of request, before any person authorized to administer oaths, or before a person commissioned by the court to administer any necessary oath. The treaty applicable to taking depositions overseas, The Hague Convention on Taking Evidence Abroad in Civil and Commercial Matters, contains a provision allowing countries to express reservations about discovery that might be permitted in their respective country.[13] Prior to taking any discovery outside of the United States, you must check the local laws to determine if your discovery is permitted and, if so, the conditions under which you must proceed.

Ways to Assist the Court Reporter

Q 3.3.2 Should I do anything to help the court reporter?

Yes, bring a copy of the notice or subpoena to the deposition. The court reporter will need the case information for the formal transcript. Many lawyers mark the deposition notice or subpoena as an exhibit to the deposition. Doing so allows for certainty that the deposition is taking place at the time and place in the notice or subpoena. The practice also reminds the witness of the formal nature of the process.

Also bring with you names and specialized terms that may be hard for the court reporter. If you use the same court reporter, they will build such a list over time, but this is a great way to save time at your deposition. The practice will also improve the quality of the transcript.

Use of Live Transcript Feeds

Q 3.3.3 Should I follow the transcript as it is being taken?

Technology allows you to see the transcript being generated by the court reporter in real time. Whether you want to do so is purely one of personal preference. Those that prefer this ability find it convenient to quote exact testimony back to a witness. If you anticipate a need to call the court because of an issue at the deposition, the actual transcript may prove beneficial. And, some people think better when they see the answer written before them.

Trying to follow the transcript while also listening to the answers and formulating additional questions can be distracting. As we will discuss in more detail in chapter 6, listening to the answers is a very important part of the deposition process. Listening requires using more than just your ears, it requires your eyes as well. The way a witness looks when an answer is given will tell as much as the words used. Formulating questions can also be hindered by watching the question appear on the screen as you articulate it. The tendency is to rephrase the question as you speak.

Early in your deposition career, the distractions may outweigh the benefits. If you have another person attending the deposition, the real-time transcript option makes sense.

The Use of Videotape (or Other Means) to Record a Deposition

Q 3.4 Should I videotape the deposition?

The decision to videotape a deposition involves more than just whether you would like a video of the testimony. The decision to videotape a deposition sends signals to the witness and the other side. To the witness, it signals that the deposition is a very formal process. Adding a videographer and the associated equipment will fill up the deposition room. (Prior to the recent advances in camera lens technology, the videographer also brought additional lighting.) To the lawyers for the other side, the decision to videotape the deposition signals that you have a great interest in pursuing the case. They know that the videographer is an additional expense that might be foregone were you thinking of a quick settlement instead.

Putting those considerations aside, the power of the video depositions cannot be understated. Seeing the demeanor and tone of the words as well as the written word changes the meaning altogether. There is a great scene in the movie *My Cousin Vinny* where the sheriff interrogates one of the two "yutes" who confesses to shooting the store clerk:[14]

Sheriff:	When did you shoot the clerk?
Bill:	What?
Sheriff:	At what point did you shoot the clerk?
Bill:	I shot the clerk.
Sheriff:	Yes, when did you shoot him?
Bill:	I shot the clerk.

Interruption takes place.

On the written record, Bill has just confessed to shooting the clerk. But, when you watch the video,[15] a different impression arises. Bill thinks he is being questioned for shoplifting a can of tuna fish, and he does not understand that the clerk was shot. Just like the movie watcher knows that Bill is not confessing but is expressing surprise at the question being asked, so too can a juror or a judge better gauge what a witness really means with the video of the testimony.

The downside of the video deposition is the added cost. The amount at issue in the case has to justify the videographer's expense, which may be several thousand dollars for a day. Assuming the cost makes sense, include the fact that a video will be made in the deposition notice.

In your calculation of cost of the deposition, include the cost of synching the video to the written transcript. Any later display of the video can then show the written transcript at the same time as the video plays.

The Way to Use Documents

Q 3.5 What about documents I want to use in the deposition?

Technology has come a long way and will continue to do so. Today, you can bring the documents you need to examine a witness on many portable devices. Court reporters offer document hosting and display services. And tomorrow will bring other technological ways to display documents at a deposition.

Technology should be used whenever possible. But, plan ahead and assume that the technology will fail and have a backup plan.[16] You cannot cancel a deposition just because your technology failed without risking having to pay for the costs of all other parties who attended the deposition.

You should practice using the technology so that your deposition will not be unduly delayed. Delay generally benefits the witness with time to re-compose during breaks. You also must consider how the technologically aided deposition will be viewed later by a judge or jury. Particularly if the deposition is being videotaped, make sure that the technology will allow the document to be displayed simultaneously with the video.

The safest backup plan is to have paper copies of the exhibits. Have your marked-up copy and clean copies for the witness and for each party at the deposition. Yes, this may create much paper and you may have to ship the materials to the deposition in advance. The safety of having the hard copy documents available will waylay that minimal burden.[17]

Q 3.6 How do I make sure the documents are admissible?

Admissibility involves two related questions. First, is the document authentic—is it what it purports to be? Second, is the document otherwise admissible under the rules of evidence? The deposition is the best time to address both issues since you may not have another shot at the witness prior to your use of the document in motion practice, a hearing, or at trial.

Addressing these issues requires you to plan ahead. The easiest way is to secure a stipulation from the other parties that the documents will be admissible. The problem arises because most parties fail to reach such agreements until they know what documents are at issue. Parties fail to reach that position until they are preparing the joint pretrial materials. You may secure a stipulation of authenticity but not admissibility. Take what the other side will offer, recognizing that you will have to make a similar agreement.[18]

Absent agreement, you must know how to authenticate your documents and how to prove their admissibility. There are several avenues for both. Authentication can come from:

1. Direct testimony by the witness that the document is what it purports to be, based on their prior familiarity with the document;
2. Testimony from the custodian of records that the document is one of the type maintained by the party and, absent some indication of issues with the particular document showing its lack of trustworthiness;
3. Testimony by a non-expert familiar with handwriting or of an expert comparing handwriting to a known sample;
4. The document authenticates itself by a certification from public record, published in a newspaper, or other official publication; or
5. The document is over twenty years old, was found where it would be expected to be, and there are no facts suggesting suspicion about its authenticity.

Fed. R. Evid. 901.

Admissibility can turn on several factors, but the most common one is finding an exception to the hearsay rule. The statements in a document are an out-of-court statement and fall under the hearsay rule unless an exception applies.[19] The most common exception applied to documents is the business record exception in Rule 803(6). To qualify, a document must:

1. Be made at or near the time by a person with knowledge or from information transmitted by a person with knowledge;
2. Be kept in the regular course of business;
3. Be part of the regular activity of the business to make and keep the document; and
4. Be confirmed by the testimony of the custodian of the document or certified by the business that prepared the document.

Absent a stipulation, ask these questions for each document you use with a witness.

Notes to Chapter 3

1. Model Rule of Professional Responsibility 4.2 provides that "a lawyer shall not communicate about the subject of the representation with a person the lawyer knows to be represented by another lawyer in the matter. Various states have different formulations of this prohibition. And, because the question will only come up after the person you talk to has complained, it is a great practice to make it a routine question of all witnesses that you approach directly."

2. *See* Rule 45(a)(3) ("An attorney also may issue and sign a subpoena if the attorney is authorized to practice in the issuing court.").

3. "Serving a subpoena requires delivering a copy to the named person . . ." FED. R. CIV. P. 45(b)(1).

4. Witnesses are to receive $40 per day of testimony and also may be compensated for time required to travel to the deposition location. 28 U.S.C. § 1821(b). The witness is also entitled to reasonable travel expenses that vary depending on the means of travel. The basic rule is that the witness is allowed the same reimbursement that the General Services Administration allows for federal employees. Currently, a witness travelling by car is entitled to 54 cents per mile. http://www.gsa.gov/portal/content/100715.

5. Appendix A contains a section on the proper place for a deposition under individual state rules.

6. Appendix A contains a list of the state provisions providing for Rule 30(b)(6) depositions.

7. QBE Ins. Corp. v. Jorda Enters., Inc., 277 F.R.D. 676 (S.D. Fla. 2012).

8. Prior to the recent amendments, Rule 26(b)(2)(C) provided the court could limit discovery in several situations, including "(iii) the burden or expense of the proposed discovery outweighs its likely benefit, considering the needs of the case, the amount in controversy, the parties' resources, the importance of the issues at stake in the action, and the importance of the discovery in resolving the issues."

9. The parties will sometimes agree in advance that depositions of their respective witnesses will take place at their lawyers' offices. While this might be inconvenient for the lawyer taking the deposition, the advantages of certainty of location and access to potential information that might arise offset the minor inconvenience of travel.

10. In case of any issues arising as to time or location, you will want the new notice or subpoena for the court's review. And, the revised notice removes any doubt as to the new time and/or location for the deposition. So, always issue a revised notice/subpoena for any material changes.

11. Most states permit notaries to swear in witnesses, and most court reporters are also notaries.

12. Rule 29(a) allows the party to stipulate that a deposition may be taken before any person so long as the parties stipulate to that person.

13. Several signatories to the Hague Convention were concerned about the breadth of discovery allowed in the United States and adopted the Convention only after limiting the possible scope of discovery. China, for example, will not allow any deposition of one of its citizens in a foreign matter, even if voluntary, absent full compliance with the Hague Convention protocols. Luckily, the State Department maintains a web page with current information on what is allowed in any country. *See* https://travel.state.gov/content/travel/en/legal-considerations/judicial/country.html.

14. A 1992 film from 20th Century Fox, *My Cousin Vinny*, has a number of scenes useful to teaching trial advocacy.

15. https://www.youtube.com/watch?v=tCoRww3Px-g.

16. Having a backup plan is good advice for any event relying on technology. Judges can get impatient waiting for an attorney to solve a technological issue.

17. See chapter 4 for a discussion of ways to organize documents.

18. One of the most often cited idioms applicable to litigation practice is "what's good for the goose is good for the gander." Shortened, this becomes the Goose Gander Rule and means you should not ask for things from the other side that you are not willing to give them.

19. Hearsay is a "statement, other than one made by the declarant while testifying at trial or hearing, offered in evidence to prove the truth of the matter asserted." FED. R. EVID. 801. Rule 801 goes on to identify a number of statements that are not hearsay. Rule 802 states that hearsay is not admissible unless it meets an exception. Rules 803 and 804 then provide a number of exceptions to the hearsay rule. Rule 803(6) provides an exception for "business records."

4

Preparing to Take the Deposition

The actual process of asking questions of a witness takes considerable preparation time, which lawyers often underestimate. Experience with taking depositions helps reduce the time required, but never forget that preparation is a labor intensive activity. The best deposition takers have a complete command of the facts of the case. Those talented takers also know the role the particular witness plays in the case.

This intensive preparation allows the questioner to know the right deposition purposes to pursue. And, it permits the creation of the proper goals for the deposition. Without the preparation, the examiner must engage in guess work that may lead to missing critical information from a particular witness.

Too often, lawyers make assumptions about what a witness will know about the case and only explore those assumptions. Without knowing they are doing so, these lawyers cut themselves off from potentially vital information—information that might only arise at trial. Avoid these surprises by allowing your preparation to inform you of the witness's likely role and then confirm that role by the questions you ask.

Starting the Preparation for the Deposition

Q 4.1 How do I get ready for a deposition?

Be prepared to devote significant time to the preparation process. Before you take anyone's deposition, you must have a command of the overall facts of the case, the witness's role, and how the witness fits with your overall case theme. You will have lots of materials to review—documents, depositions, interview notes, the Internet, and your client's information on the witness. Do not leave out any source of potential information. Your goal should be to have the best possible understanding of the information, good and bad, that the witness can bring to the issues in the case.

The information reviewed and collected will form the basis of your deposition outline. And, the outline forms the basis of your questioning of the witness. Starting with the questions without doing the preparation will lead to a deposition that only confirms facts you already know. While that might be useful, the witness may leave the deposition room with information you need to know. Preparation is the best way to prevent that from happening.

Q 4.1.1 Why do I need to do that much preparation?

Time limitations require that deposition questions be focused on productive areas. In most jurisdictions, you know longer have the luxury of spending time during the deposition trying to figure out the areas to explore. Knowledge also allows you to know when the witness is trying to dodge your questions, or even lying. Knowledge also allows you to refresh the recollection of a witness struggling to remember details. Finally, the preparation process allows you to gauge the importance of the witness to the overall story line and allows you to determine the purposes of the deposition before the first question.

Q 4.1.2 How do you prepare for the person to be deposed?

Start by learning as much as you can about the person's job and responsibilities. If he works for a corporation that is involved, place the witness on the corporate organization chart. Find out about his educational background. Your client may provide some of this information, but still look on the Internet to see what is available. You should not, however, intrude on private networks or become friends on Facebook, Twitter, or similar social media cites, as this could violate rules of professional conduct.[1] Once you know the publicly available information, it is time to look for the case-specific data. What role did your witness play in the events leading to the litigation? Was the witness a decision maker? Did the witness harbor doubts about the issues? What was the witness's relationship with other case players? What have other deponents said about this witness?

Delving into the discovery—documents and interrogatory responses—will develop perspective on how to approach the witness. Will the witness be the only source of information on certain events? If so, more care and time will be spent exploring that event. If not, does the witness confirm or contradict the account of others? Should you try to build up or undercut the witness's recollection of events?

These questions form the fundamental building blocks of deposition preparation. Your answers mold the scope of the outline and the selection of documents to be used. These questions also guide your decision whether to spend time in discovery mode or in seeking admissions and limiting testimony.

Reviewing the Relevant Documents

Q 4.1.3 How should the documents be reviewed?

The size of the document production will guide the review process more than any other item. Large collections will be reviewed by key words and by author. Smaller collections will all be reviewed by hand. If the key word or other technological method of review is employed, the person asking the questions must still review the selected documents to determine those documents that might be needed at the deposition. Only a personal document review allows the questioner to determine the value of the document and how it might be used.

Q 4.1.4 What should I look for in a document?

Documents can be used for several purposes in a deposition. First, the documents can assist an honest witness in explaining important case information. The documents may help fill in a key event or place an event on a timeline properly. The documents may also be useful in explaining key relationships among parties to the case.

Documents may also provide support for your case theory. And, a case theory supported by documents from the other side has greater believability. Documents may also undermine the witness's testimony—directly by impeachment or indirectly by creating a conflict with the story being told by the witness. As an example, suppose the document contains the exact opposite statement from the witness's deposition testimony. This creates the perfect impeachment scenario. If the document merely records the contradictory recollection of another witness, the challenge to the witness is indirect. In the indirect case, you will want to see what testimony the witness will give you that bolsters the contradictory statement. This information may come from the other party's ability to view those events from their position of authority in the company, or from their superior expertise.

At the time of review, you will not know how the document will be best used nor will you know the explanation the witness may give relating to the document. But, you will know that the document relates to your case and to your witness. You will move the document to the witness preparation folder.

Identify the Witness's Role in the Case

Q 4.1.5 How do I know how the witness fits into the case story?

First, you must have a very good understanding of your client's version of the events preceding the litigation. This will not happen in a single meeting. It will evolve over time as you uncover additional bits of information from your other efforts to learn about the case. While it doesn't work for every case, you might develop a key event timeline that allows you to track the information as you learn it. But, track more than just the event on the timeline—track the people involved. Stories are told by people. And, add the key documents that corroborate or contradict the key events. You will be a long way ahead of the trial preparation process if you update your timeline regularly.

As you add people to the timeline, build a separate chart of key players, on which you can note the information you learn from each about the witness's role—employer, title position, and connection to the information you need for the case.[2] Information will come from a variety of sources, including your client and the documents both sides produce.

For each person you add, ask yourself if that person has information you need for case development. If yes, then ask yourself if the witness will speak to you without need of a deposition, assuming the witness is not represented by counsel or is not an employee of a corporate defendant that is represented by counsel. If the witness is not represented and is willing to talk to you outside of a formal deposition, then go interview him or her and base your deposition decision on the interview results. If the witness will not speak with you or is represented by counsel, the deposition calculus (to depose or not) requires consideration of:

- Is the prospective witness the only person capable of testifying about an event?
- Does the prospective witness have any reason to slant the version of events for one side?
- Are there documents that compel the prospective witness to tell the story in only one manner?

- Is the prospective witness likely to be a key story teller for the other side so you must hear the story before trial?
- Will the prospective witness corroborate key elements of your view of the case?

Answering these questions will tell you whether deposing the witness makes sense given the limited number of depositions that may be available to you.

Methods to Organize Your Materials

Q 4.2 What are the best methods of organizing your witness preparation materials?

Over time you will develop a preference for how to organize your deposition preparation materials. Often the method you select will vary with the facts. Does the story depend solely on a chronology? Does the story vary more by specific events than by time? Is there an overlap between these two? How large is the universe of documents? What follows are suggested approaches to consider as you figure out your own particular approach.

If your case story follows a chronology, then a chronological organization of all the documents you are considering for the deposition is the easiest and makes the most sense. The chronological approach ensures that you will not skip any key dates in the story.

The chronological approach may not be ideal for a case with several events that are important, however, as that approach may cause you to lose track of the key events. In such cases, you may want to arrange the documents topically. Grouping all documents by topic insures that you have all the materials related to that topic together. But what if a single document relates to more than one topic? For example, a hospital admitting report might relate to injury, but it might also contain information relating to causation. Your system (manual or electronic) should allow you to tag multiple topics. Avoid the tendency to make extra copies of documents with multiple topics. The resulting geometric increase in the size of the documents for the deposition can overwhelm. Once a document is marked as an exhibit, the same exhibit can be used for multiple questions relating to different topics. How to use documents in the deposition will be discussed in chapter 5.

Yet a third approach is to construct a hybrid of the chronological and topical methods. Within each topic area, the documents can be arranged chronologically, or you can create subtopics.

Q 4.3 Are there other items to consider in the preparation process?

Maybe. Each case is different and may raise different items that must be reviewed prior to developing the actual deposition outline. Once you have exhausted the documents, your client, and the Internet, is there anything else you should do? Ask your colleagues for additional ideas. For some cases, others might suggest looking at textbooks, consulting experts, or something else entirely. The point is that, consistent with the terms of any protective order, you are not limited to your own ingenuity to identify sources that will help prepare for a deposition.[3]

Preparing the Deposition Outline

Q 4.4 I have done the preparation, how do I put together a deposition outline?

What may be missed by this question is that the goal is to prepare an outline and not a list of questions to ask. Why? Preparing written questions in advance detracts from your ability to listen to the witness and adapt your questions in response to the witness's testimony. The brain works much faster than the witness's ability to speak, creating lots of idle time. The brain will look for places to wander and a list of questions provides the perfect temptation. And, while you think about that next question, the witness may reveal an important detail, not already in your list of questions, you may well miss.

Q 4.4.1 OK, so how do I develop the outline?

Put at the top of the outline a reminder to swear in the witness. Most court reporters will do this automatically, but occasionally it is forgotten.[4] While there may be arguments that can be made that the unsworn testimony remains useable, the best practice is to avoid the issue by making a note to yourself to swear in the witness in every outline you create.

Next on the list is to make sure that the witness identifies himself by his full name. Most deposition takers also ask the witness to spell his or her name to avoid any confusion. As part of this process, you also want the witness to provide an address, preferably home address, where he or she can later be found if necessary. Why? Again, you may never need the information, but if you are looking to subpoena the witness for trial, the address will come in handy. And, the witness identification comes in handy if there is ever a dispute about the witness's identity.

The final general category that should be included in all outlines is called admonitions. Admonitions are instructions to the witness about how the deposition process will proceed. But, admonitions, done properly, also lay the foundation for impeachment. We will discuss admonitions in greater detail in chapter 5. For now, make a note in the outline to have a brief discussion with the witness about the rules of the deposition.

Q 4.4.2 Now that I have these general matters in the outline, what do I do next?

Now it is time to decide on the topics you want to address with this witness. Take a blank piece of paper and start a list—don't worry about any order—of topics that come to mind for this witness. Keep this list close as you work on the deposition outline. Invariably, developing the outline will cause new topics to arise that must find their way onto the list. As you make the list, try to be over-inclusive. You can always remove items later. Think of the process as a brainstorming session. Like all brainstorming sessions, do not criticize your ideas as you put them on the list. The goal is to get as many items as you can. And, do not limit yourself to your own imagination—ask others. Once you have your list, you can use it as the starting point for every deposition in the case.

Next, take an item on the list and start a new list. Decide what you would like to know about the item you selected—think in terms of "who, what, when, why, and how" topics. You may also need to confirm information because you know the only other source of the information is your client.[5] Make a separate list of those matters. Repeat the process for each item on the main list.

Finally, decide on the priority of the items you selected for the specific witness you are about to depose. Remember, you may have a time limit and not be able to address all topics in your outline with a particular witness. One way to assess the priority of a topic with a particular witness is to use that witness's role in the case as a guide. Another approach to prioritization focuses on whether there are other witnesses with a better opportunity to observe the matters at issue. Yet another approach turns on whether you are seeking to gain information on a topic or are trying to limit the witness's ability to testify about a matter. If it is the latter, you may achieve that goal in far less time by concentrating on the ability of the witness to observe events, gain acknowledgment that another witness had a better viewpoint, or agree that the witness has some obvious bias.

Even with your rough priority of topics established, further opportunities to improve your organization exist. Will you proceed topically? Chronologically? Does a random approach seem right for this witness? As a practical matter, there is no rule that requires you to ask questions in any order. Each approach has advantages and disadvantages. The topical and chronological approaches both send the witness fairly good signals of what is coming and what is likely completed as the deposition progresses. Either approach may work well with a witness that has no incentive to keep information from you, but not so well from a witness with an incentive to keep information close.

Some questioners will always begin the deposition with background questions to build rapport with the witness. These questioners believe that a witness allowed to talk about themselves first will be more forthcoming as the topics move into those that are case-specific. These questioners seek to have the witness at ease throughout the process. Other questioners believe that it is better to keep the witness off guard by constantly changing topics and circling back to topics already covered.

As you think about your approach to a particular witness, remember that you never have a second chance to make a first impression. Applied to depositions, this philosophy often attributed to Will Rogers means that an aggressive approach towards the witness can never be recalled. As we will discuss in chapter 10 on defending depositions, the witness has been told that you represent the forces of evil, or a close approximation thereof, and are not their friend. As soon as you confirm that observation, the hope of a cooperative witness disappears.

If you are looking for a general rule, start the deposition with the general admonitions, hit the witness's background enough to establish his or her connection to the case, and then try to discover as much information from the witness as you can. Only after you have exhausted your discovery efforts should you move to theory testing and other deposition purposes.

Adding Documents to the Deposition Outline

Q 4.4.3 How do I work the documents into the outline?

You have reviewed lots of documents connected to your case. Now you must select those that matter for the witness. How? There are several guides you may use. First, look for documents that the witness authored, received, or is mentioned somewhere in the text. Second, ask yourself if the document matches any of the topics that you created as a priority. If so, make a note of the document and the priority issue to which it applies. Third, ask if the document might be useful to impeach the witness on an important point. Remember that the best impeachment comes from a document written by the witness. At the deposition phase, any statement to the contrary may undercut the witness's testimony.

Once you have set aside a subset of documents for the witness, the hard process of selecting the documents that must be available in the deposition room begins. Start with the stack of documents you have tagged as important to a priority issue for the witness.[6] In each category, force rank the documents. Which documents make the point? Which are more attenuated? Which ones will the witness be able to avoid in some fashion? Use the answers to these questions to select the ones you want to use from the documents you might use depending on the witness's testimony.

Now, it is time to come up with a reference system. Your system can be as simple as assigning each priority category a letter or a number and then numbering each document in that category. Or you can develop a system as complicated as that used by the Library of Congress. The secret is that each document has a unique identifier linked to the priority topic applicable to that document. All that matters is that you have a system that will allow you to find a document on a moment's notice without looking through them all. Some documents may well be treasure troves of information and useful to a variety of your priority topics. Resist the temptation to give that document multiple numbers or create multiple copies of it. Just use the first number you give that document in each priority category.

Once you have your document organization system established, it's time to head back to the outline. With each document in hand, find the place in your outline where the document is most likely to come up. Make a note of the document number in the outline with a note why you think the document is relevant. The note is important because you may well forget the specific details of each document selected.

Q 4.5 How will you know whether to use the documents at the deposition?

Documents are used for several reasons during the deposition process. Some documents are fundamental to your case theory and need to be admissible at trial. Whether or not you have substantive questions about those documents, you will want to lay the foundation for their admission with the right witness. Documents that constitute the contract at issue fall in this category.

For other documents, more strategic questions must be addressed. Sometimes using a document is a good way to show the witness you have spent the time to prepare for the deposition and they cannot hide key information from you. This tactic works early in the deposition and can help a reluctant witness testify more fully. Sometimes you need the document to impeach a witness that has made a statement that hurts your case. Other times the document allows you to undermine the witness's credibility or establish their bias against your side of the case.

Many documents are used to complete the story. Witnesses will forget important details that documents can refresh. Or witnesses can try to withhold key facts that the documents can reveal. Deciding on when, or whether, to use the documents for any of these reasons depends on what the witness says, your assessment of the witness's attitude, and where you are in the deposition day. Many questioners will use the first half of the deposition to collect the witness's testimony without the assistance of documents and then return to the same topics with the documents later in the deposition. This approach can waste a lot of time and result in many "I don't recall" answers. For most witnesses, use the documents as the topics come up if using the document will improve the deposition to your benefit.

Q 4.5.1 Shouldn't I use all the documents I brought to the deposition?

No. Just because you brought a document to the deposition does not mean it must be used.[7] As you listen to the witness during the deposition you will learn that several pre-deposition assumptions were wrong. Not all topics you thought were important to address with the witness will remain important. And, new topics are likely to develop as you listen. Because you prepared for discovery before selecting this witness, these new topics will not catch you by surprise. You may not have all the documents with you at the deposition, but you will at least be able to question the witness on the areas that need exploration.[8]

Notes to Chapter 4

1. Model Rules of Professional Conduct Rule 4.2 provides: "In representing a client, a lawyer shall not communicate about the subject of the representation with a person the lawyer knows to be represented by another lawyer in the matter, unless the lawyer has the consent of the other lawyer or is authorized to do so by law or a court order." *See, e.g.*, Philadelphia Bar Ass'n Prof'l Guidance Comm. Op. 2009-02; New York Bar Ass'n Ethics Op. 2010-02; New York State Bar Ass'n Ethics Op. 843 (2010); New Hampshire Bar Ass'n Ethics Comm. Op. 2012-13/05; San Diego County Ethics Op. 2011-2.

2. It is beyond the scope of this book to discuss trial preparation in detail, but the process of conducting deposition intertwines with trial often. Remember that all cases should be handled from the very beginning as if they are headed to trial. Discovery will be more productive if it focuses on items that you know you will need to try the case. If you do not know what those items are, ask others with more experience to give you some advice.

3. Textbooks and experts will come in handy for deposing the other side's experts, but they may also be useful ways to provide background information that will make your questioning of the fact witnesses more productive. Suppose that one of the issues in the case involved the method used to calculate an accounting reserve. Unless you studied accounting, and remember what you studied, an expert can give you the background information you need to ask questions about the process.

4. Rule 603 of the Federal Rules of Evidence provides: "Before testifying, every witness shall be required to declare that the witness will testify truthfully, by oath or affirmation administered in a form calculated to awaken the witness' conscience and impress the witness with the duty to do so." "The twofold purpose of the oath is to bind the conscience of the witness and make him amenable to prosecution if he gives perjured testimony." Wilcoxon v. United States, 231 F.2d 384, 386 (10th Cir. 1956).

5. The ability to persuade with evidence from your client places a lot of importance on the assessment of the client's credibility. You can bolster that credibility assessment by having key parts of the story confirmed by the testimony of others.

6. Of course, the review and marking process may all be done electronically on a review platform. Even so, remember that you will want hard copy documents for the deposition!

7. Of course, there is a terrible tendency to use the exhibits just to avoid the hassle of carrying the unused copies back to your office. Consider carefully the impact of using a document on the witness and on your case before marking it as an exhibit.

8. You can also use a break to seek to have a colleague send you a few of the more important documents that you might need for a break. As long as you keep the number of documents to a manageable size, you should be able to get copies printed and proceed with the deposition on those topics as well.

5

The Deposition Day

The hard work of preparation is over and the deposition day has arrived. Lawyers can become their own worst enemy. Lawyers will often become nervous about taking the deposition. Other lawyers will focus more on trying to impress the other lawyers in the room. The well-prepared lawyer will focus on the witness. After all, the witness's statements taken on the deposition record are all that matter that day. That testimony is all that can have any future value in the case. When the big day arrives, take a deep breath, relax, and focus on the witness to the exclusion of all others in the room.

The Last Minute Details Before the Deposition

Q 5.1 What do I do the week before the deposition begins?

Make sure you have spoken to your court reporter a few days before the deposition. As the party taking the deposition, arranging the court reporter and videographer, if videotaping is occurring, is your responsibility. Take the time to confirm the deposition day, time, and location. Give the court reporter a way to contact you if an emergency occurs, and make sure that you know the court reporter's name and can contact him or her. If the deposition is to be videotaped and the videographer is not associated with the court reporter, you must contact that person as well.

Finish your outline. Then, using your unique numbering system, make sure that you have your documents organized in your anticipated order of use. Realize that the actual order of use will vary as the deposition proceeds. You will decide not to use certain documents with the witness based on testimony already given and you may well use a document out of order. When you go out of order, your numbering system will allow you to quickly find the document you wish to use. If you are using the hard copy of documents method, you will place at least three copies of each document in a manila folder marked with your numbering system. Why three copies? You need one for the court reporter to mark and show to the witness, one for counsel representing the witness, and a copy for any emergency need that arises. Of course, in a multiple-party case, you will need copies for the lawyers representing each party.

Make sure you are up to date on all other discovery issues. If there is an ongoing discovery dispute, ask yourself if the witness might have information relevant to that dispute. Will the witness know where documents are located? How about who to ask for those documents? If it is at all likely, add these areas to your outline.

As part of that process, check all other depositions taken in your case. You will want to note any testimony where another witness has spoken about the witness you are about to depose or areas where you expect your witness to also testify. This testimony may lead to other questions to add to your outline. Copy the testimony into your outline. Having the testimony in your outline will make it easier to check the consistency of your witness's testimony. If there is an inconsistency, you may challenge your witness or you may save the challenge for trial. Several considerations go into making this decision. How likely is the case to go to trial? How good a witness is the source of the inconsistent testimony? Has the witness shown a tendency to change testimony based on statements of others? Which version of events helps your case the most? Assuming the inconsistency is helpful to your side, you need to ask questions that will bolster the testimony of your witness. Affirm the observation or opinion based upon their opportunity to observe events, confirming documents, or any other confirming source.

Make sure your outline has plenty of white space for you to add additional thoughts and ideas as you review the outline. Every time you look at the outline you will think of some other matter to address. As you finalize the outline, take one more opportunity to contact other members of your team to ask again for further thoughts on items to be covered. This provides an opportunity to discuss how you plan to approach the most difficult issues. Discussing these matters allows you to refine your approach and to see possible problems with your approach. You may also learn of additional relevant facts. Your deposition preparation will be enhanced by the process.

Put the outline in a small notebook. If the outline is more than a few pages, include dividers that break up the outline by subjects. Assuming a small enough collection of documents, you can place your marked-up copy of the documents in the notebook behind the appropriate tab or you may keep your marked-up copy in front of the manila folder with the document copies. While there are advantages to both methods, putting the key documents in the binder makes it easier to review those documents right before the deposition.

Deposition Day Tasks

Q 5.2 What should I do the day of the deposition?

Eat a big breakfast. You may find the lunch break too short for you to eat and prepare for the afternoon session. Arrive early. If the location of the deposition is not your office, arrive at least thirty minutes early. You will need the time to familiarize yourself with the surroundings, including the location of restrooms, and to organize your materials. Ensure that your documents are readily accessible. Then, spend a few minutes before the witness arrives thinking through the plan for the start of the deposition. Just remember that no plan survives first contact with the enemy.[1] Listen to the witness and adapt your plan and your questions accordingly.

Starting the Deposition

Q 5.2.1 They are ready to start the deposition, what do I do?

Take a deep breath, relax, and let your preparation take over. By looking at the outline, you know that you will make sure the witness is sworn in and that you will ask the witness to state their name, having them spell it for clarity, and get the witness's address. Next, you will want to make sure there is an understanding of whether there are any special rules that will govern the proceeding.

Q 5.2.2 What types of special rules should I worry about?

Two topics are raised most often—what types of objections must be made, and before whom the witness can have his signature to the final transcript notarized. The rules that govern the deposition you are taking normally have default provisions that control. Rule 29 of the Federal Rules of Civil Procedure provides that the parties may modify rules relating to discovery, with certain exceptions, by stipulation.[2]

Objections by defending lawyers can be a major interruption to the deposition flow. To avoid the interference, lawyers may stipulate that only objections to the form of the question may be allowed. Several jurisdictions have imposed this requirement. Texas attorneys are limited to "Objection, leading" and "Objection, form."[3] All other objections are preserved by rule. The theory behind these rules is that an objection to the form of the question allows the questioner to correct the issue while the witness is present.

By stipulation, however, you can agree that all objections will be preserved and that none must be raised during the deposition. The decision to do so depends from the questioner's perspective on the confidence they have in asking non-objectionable questions and the interference expected from the defending lawyer. On the defending side, the lawyer may not want to agree to such a stipulation because he may believe he needs to signal his witness when a tricky question has been asked.

Making sure the witness can sign the deposition before any notary lacks controversy. Rule 30(e) of the Federal Rules of Civil Procedure says that the witness or a party may request prior to the end of the deposition the right to review the transcript and make changes. The witness must list the changes, the reasons the change is being made, and sign that statement.

Avoid the Usual Stipulations

Q 5.2.3 I was just asked to agree to the "usual stipulations" . . . what should I do?

Don't agree. What are the usual stipulations? When asked, almost no one can provide you with a list of the stipulations. And, the list will vary from lawyer to lawyer and from court reporter to court reporter. Younger lawyers will often feel a need to agree to the "usual" stipulations as a way of looking knowledgeable. The new guy on the block wants to fit in. But, the danger comes from agreeing to stipulations you do not understand. When asked this question, be polite and ask what the "usual" stipulations are in that person's mind. Tell them you want to avoid any ambiguity later and would like to be sure that everyone is clear. Perhaps you want to help the court reporter comply with their duty under Rule 30(b)(5)(C) to "set out any stipulations made by the attorneys about custody of the transcript or recording and of the exhibits, or about any other pertinent matters." Or you can simply say, we will conduct this deposition under the rules of civil procedure of either your state or the federal rules. The rules provide a clear guide how the deposition should be conducted.

Admonitions to the Witness

Q 5.3 The witness is sworn, has identified himself, and has given his address . . . now what?

Now you have complete discretion how to proceed. You may go directly into substantive questioning or you can give the witness a series of admonitions. Admonitions are a set of instructions to the witness about the deposition process. While making sure the witness understands how the deposition works is important, the admonitions, properly done, also provide a framework to improve impeachment at trial. They should not be given simply for drill. Admonitions are where you begin trying to build rapport with the witness. You will use the admonitions to suggest that you want to conduct the deposition fairly, seeking only to gain the knowledge the witness has relevant to your case.

There are many different admonitions you may select. What follows is a discussion of several admonitions and their connection to later impeachment:

1. Make sure the witness understands that she is under oath and giving testimony just as if she was testifying before the judge and, if applicable, jury. How? Ask something like, "Madam, you understand that you have taken an oath to testify truthfully here today? You also understand that today's testimony is just as if it were being given in a court of law? You understand that the oath you have taken carries with it the same penalties for perjury?" Why remind the witness she is under oath? If you need to impeach the witness, you will want to go back to this question-and-answer series so the witness at trial, and the jury, are reminded that the rules of the deposition were clear.

2. Explain the role of the court reporter. Make sure the witness knows the court reporter will take down everything said by everyone in the room. And, explain why this is important to the deposition testimony. How? Ask the witness something like this, "You understand the court reporter is here to take down everything that is said today? We want to make sure that she can record your testimony correctly, right? To help the reporter, will you agree to answer each question verbally? Will it be OK, if you forget, for me to ask you whether your answer was a yes or a no? And to avoid confusion, we have to watch about talking at the same time. I'll agree to let you finish an answer, and will you agree to let me finish my question before you start giving an answer?" What is the purpose of these questions? You want no key answer to be recorded as "witness nods head." The witness will later argue that he was shaking his head and not nodding when you try to impeach the testimony at trial. You also want to make sure the witness cannot later argue that you did not give him a complete opportunity to answer the questions.

3. Tell the witness to let you know if there is any confusion about your question. How? Try something like this, "Sir, if you do not understand any of my questions, will you agree to let me know that you don't? Will you also agree to tell me the problem you are having with the question?" The purpose of these questions is to short circuit the later argument that the witness was confused about the question you asked. Avoid the temptation to ask the witness if you can assume he understood your question if he fails to say anything. Assumptions are just that, and the answer will not increase your impeachment impact at trial.

4. Tell the witness not to speculate. How? Ask something like this, "Sir, because you are under oath, will you agree that the answers you give me will be to the best of your knowledge? Will you also agree not to guess or speculate about an answer unless I ask you to do so?" Wait, don't you want the witness to speculate as long at the speculation helps your case? Sure

you do, but you also want to use the answer later. If the witness later testifies that the answer was just a guess, you can remind him that he agreed not to do that during the deposition. And, you can take comfort knowing that witnesses forget your instructions to them anyway.

5. Assure the witness she may ask for a break whenever she needs one. How would you do that? Try, "Madam, my practice is to try to break every hour, but if you need a break sooner than that will you agree to let me know? The only thing I ask is that you answer any question that I have asked before we break, is that agreeable?" Don't you want to wear down the witness? Maybe you do, but what you really want is the ability to remind the witness, who later claims to have made a statement at the deposition because she was exhausted, that she had the right to ask for breaks whenever she wanted.

6. Ask the witness if there is any reason the deposition should not proceed as all parties have agreed. You might ask: "Witness, I know I have covered a number of items with you already, but is there any reason you can think of why you cannot give truthful answers to the questions asked of you today?" This catch-all question avoids a later claim by the witness that he or she was affected by some malady you failed to ask about directly. A common question to ask is whether the witness is taking any medications, or other substance, that might impair his or her ability to answer questions truthfully. And if you get a positive answer, be prepared to discuss with the defending lawyer whether the deposition may proceed. In the absence of an agreement, the deposition will need to be postponed until the issue can be resolved.

Q 5.3.1 What are the typical problems lawyers encounter during the admonition phase?

Some lawyers are very nervous at the start of the deposition. They are worried that the deposition will not produce the information needed to aid their side of the case or they are simply new at the discovery process and afraid they will make mistakes. Whatever the cause, nervousness can make lawyers rush through their list of admonitions—often running several together. The result is that the witness is never asked to agree with the admonition being given. Each admonition must have a separate acknowledgment from the witness. The separate acknowledgment allows the admonition to be later used against the witness when he or she seeks to retreat from the deposition testimony. An admonition with no corresponding acceptance by the witness will be useless in that process.

Besides nerves, some lawyers believe that the admonitions are nothing more than a waste of time. Most cases settle. There will likely be no need to ever use the admonitions. And, those admonitions take away from getting to substantive information faster. Two responses are in order. First, the only sure way to make sure a case settles on favorable terms is to treat every case as if it will be the one that gets tried. Second, if you follow the first approach, you will be ready to impeach the witness with their deposition.

Q 5.3.2 How would I use the admonitions during a later impeachment process?

Most lawyers fail to take the time to make an impeachment memorable for the trier of fact. Below is an example of how to use the admonitions to create a more effective impeachment. Assume for this example that the witness testified on deposition that the traffic light was red at the time of the accident, but at trial changes the answer to say the light was green. You might ask questions like this:

Q. You testified today that the light was green, is that right?

Q. Do you want to change that answer?

Q. You recall I [or someone else on your side of the case] took your deposition in this case?

Q. You were sworn to tell the truth during that deposition?

Q. And you remember that I told you to tell me if any of my questions needed clarification?

Q. You agreed you would tell me if you did not understand my question?

Q. Remember I asked if there was any reason you could not tell the truth in answer to my questions at the deposition?

Q. You told me you could do so that day, didn't you?

Q. The deposition was taken only six months after the accident, wasn't it?

Q. Let me hand you a copy of your deposition, marked as Exhibit X for identification. You recognize this as a copy of your deposition?

Q. In fact, if you flip to the end of the document, that is your signature on page 253, isn't it?

Q. Now, if I could direct your attention to page 12, line 10 of that deposition, do you see where I asked you the question, "what color was the light at the time of the accident?" Will you please read your response, "the light was green"?[4]

Depending on the answers you receive, you may want to add questions relating to other deposition admonitions or rules. Sometimes, you will want to remind the witness that he reviewed and changed any answers he gave at the deposition and then note he did not change this answer.

After the Admonitions

Q 5.4 After the admonitions, what's next?

Now, it is time to ask your substantive questions. By now, the witness has indicated a style of answering questions. And, perhaps the questioner has relaxed enough to turn to substantive areas. The next chapter will focus on how those questions should be structured.

Notes to Chapter 5

1. A reference most often attributed to German Field Marshall Helmuth Karl Bernhard Graf von Moltke.

2. Rule 29 requires any stipulation that will extend the time for any type of discovery must have court approval if it will interfere with any existing discovery deadline or a hearing or trial date. FED. R. CIV. P. 29(b).

3. TEX. R. CIV. P. 199.5(e).

4. There is no particular magic to the format of these questions at trial. They are offered as a means to see that admonitions only have later value if you secure an agreement to abide by them at the deposition. Depending on the witness, you might elect to read the answer yourself so that you can read it clearly and with appropriate emphasis.

6

The Form of the Question Matters

The way questions are phrased matters. By manipulating the form of the question and the question's structure, different results can be achieved. Some forms of questions encourage discussion. Other forms of questions seek to limit conversation. The key is to structure questions in a way that achieves the result desired.

Lawyers often speak of controlling the witness during an examination. Most lawyers use that phrase to describe a way of limiting the answers that come from the witness. More skillful lawyers know that true witness control sometimes means the exact opposite. Instead of being limited in their testimony, the question will encourage a more fulsome discussion of the issue. When the purpose is to discover the other side's strengths and weaknesses, the examiner must be facile at both types of questioning.

Varying the Question Form

Q 6.1 Should I change the form of the questions during a deposition?

Yes. The form of the question will vary with the purpose you are trying to achieve with the question. Earlier, we discussed the different purposes for a deposition. You will also want to vary the form of your questions as you change purposes.

Q 6.1.1 What forms of questions are available?

Questions fall into two broad categories—open ended or closed ended. Open ended questions encourage the witness to talk and to answer in his or her own words. The open ended question tries to learn how a witness will describe events. Those descriptions may provide the questioner with new information and will raise additional areas for further questioning. When asking open ended questions, the lawyer must exhaust the information being provided by the witness. One technique for doing so is called the "funnel approach." Closed ended questions achieve the reverse, limiting the witness's answers and using words selected by the questioner. The closed ended question tries to seek the witness's agreement with the way the lawyer has described events. The questioner will learn no new information with a closed ended question nor will there be any new areas requiring additional questions.

Q 6.1.2 How do I know whether to ask an open ended or a closed ended question?

Open ended questions are best used when introducing a new topic to the witness. As you introduce the topic, you use the open ended approach to let the witness tell you as much about the topic as he or she can. Open ended questions are the hallmark of questions seeking to fulfill the discovery purpose of the deposition. Once you think you have gotten all the information that the witness has to give you, you will shift to the closed ended question. Closed ended questions seek confirmation of one specific piece of information and are best used for testing theories and gaining admissions.

But, there will be times in the theory testing/admission gaining phase of the deposition where you may need to open up the questions. When the witness is not answering your closed ended questions the way you anticipate or your theory is not being proven, it may be time to open up the questions to find out what is preventing the witness from giving you the answers you seek.

Impact of Shifting to Closed Ended Questions

Q 6.1.3 Can you give us an example of how to reopen the questions?

Sure, but before doing that, remember that asking closed ended questions affects the witness. As you target in on admissions, the tone of the deposition changes from a friendly effort to find out what the witness knows to one focused on scoring points for your case. Seeking to score points almost always raises the questioner's energy levels and can put the witness on the defensive. The witness sees the side of you that his lawyer told him to expect in their preparation session. This recognition by the witness makes it difficult to switch back and forth between the discovery mode and the admission/theory testing mode.

With that caution, assume we are representing the plaintiff in an automobile intersection collision case. After concluding what we think is the discovery phase, we seek to prove that the defendant ran the red light, with an admission by the defendant to prove our theory of the case. Questions might go like this:

Q. On November 12, you were driving your car on West Road?

A. Yes I was.

Q. You were headed in an easterly direction on West Road?

A. True.

Q. At approximately 3:12 PM, you were approaching the intersection of West Road and Main Street?

A. I don't remember the precise time.

Q. You recall that was the time of the accident noted on the police report?

A. Yes I do.[1]

Q. You have no reason to question that the police report contains an accurate time of when you were approaching the intersection of West and Main, do you?

A. I do not.

Q. The intersection of West and Main has a red light, doesn't it?

A. Yes it does.

Q. You had been through that intersection several times prior to November 12, right?

A. Yes.

Q. In fact, the intersection of West and Main is part of your commute to work?

A. Yes.

Q. On November 12, you could clearly see the red light?

Objection; Vague

A. I am not sure I know what you mean.

Q. Was there anything that prevented you from seeing the light?

A. No there wasn't.

Q. You had a clear view of the light from your car?

A. Yes.

Q. When you went through the intersection of West and Main on November 12, the light was red, wasn't it?

A. I can't answer that question.

Q. Sir, you know that Mr. Bystander has already testified that he saw you run the red light?

A. I have heard that he made such a comment.

Q. Well then, why can't you answer my question?

A. The impact of the collision caused me not to recall the details of the collision.

When the witness failed to give us a yes to our question about the light being red, we had a choice to make. We could have continued to ask several closed ended questions designed to guess at the reasons he couldn't answer the question. We could have gotten angry and reminded him of his obligation to answer the question we asked. And, we could have reminded him he has taken an oath to testify truthfully. But, none of those strategies would have gotten us the answer we needed. They would have taken up a fair amount of our available time and frustrated us. We needed to know why he could not admit to our theory of the case. The way to learn that fact was to just ask.

Now, with the answer to the "why" question, we can reevaluate our position. Our theory, that the defendant ran the red light, is still alive. And, we now know that the defendant cannot testify differently.[2] In the real-world deposition, we would nail down his lack of memory, and establish what his last recollection of that day was and his first recollection after the collision.

The Funnel Technique

Q 6.2 Can you explain the funnel question technique?

The funnel is just a mental image of a technique to exhaust a given area of inquiry. Graphically, the funnel looks like this:

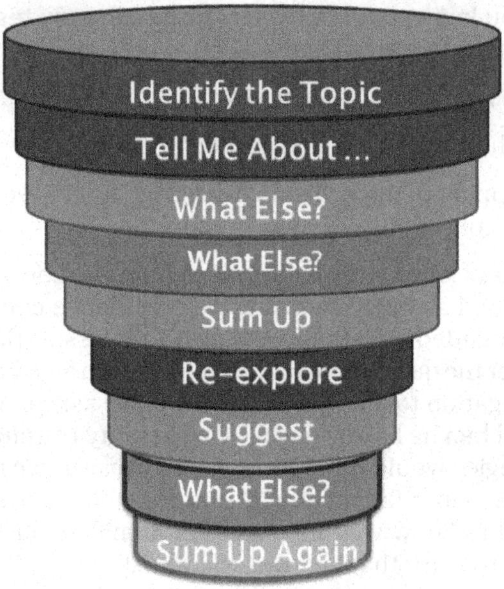

The funnel reminds you to be diligent in asking follow-up questions to exhaust the witness's knowledge on a topic.

The funnel starts by identifying the area of inquiry you desire to exhaust. Using our intersection collision case, introduced in Q 6.1.3 above, as an example, we may want to know what the plaintiff had done prior to the accident. If so, we might say, "Ms. Plaintiff, I would like to find out what you were doing before the accident occurred."[3] We have identified the area of inquiry. Now our job is to make sure we capture all of the plaintiff's testimony related to our topic.

Start that process with a broad open ended question. Continuing with our example, say, "Tell me everything you did on [day of accident] prior to the accident?" Now, we listen and take notes of everything the witness says. You may want to follow up on that answer in a few minutes. When she stops talking we have a choice to make. We can ask another question or we can use some non-verbal techniques to see if she will volunteer additional information.

Once you are convinced that the witness is done with the answer and you have decided to ask another question, ask the witness, "What else did you do?" Repeat that process until the witness tells you they have nothing else to say. Then, repeat the answers in a summary form and get the witness to agree with your description of her activities before the accident. This summary is necessary because you will want to have the testimony in a nice concise question and answer for later use. Running a funnel may take several deposition pages and it will be difficult to use that testimony effectively to support motions and at trial.

Q 6.2.1 Have we now exhausted the funnel?

It is very unlikely that this series of questions has exhausted the funnel. In the sum-up process, the witness will often think of something else to say in response to your question. When that happens, you must re-explore the topic to make sure that you have exhausted the topic from the witness's perspective. Then, you might well want to suggest some possible answers that the witness hasn't given you. For example, "Did you stop for breakfast? Coffee? Did you stop at the laundry?" If any of your suggestions prompt a positive answer, you must again proceed through the "what else?" loop. And, once you complete that loop, sum up the answer yet again.

Following Up on Answers

Q 6.2.2 During the answer, I heard several things I want to follow up on, so when do I do that?

My advice is that, if you are early in your deposition career, wait until you have exhausted the funnel to ask the follow-up questions. Why? Most lawyers get excited about following up on questions and will often forget to complete the funnel. So, be patient, complete the funnel, and then flesh out the details of the answers that relate to your case.

If you are more experienced, however, chase the answer. But, even if you are an experienced questioner, you should make a note of where you were in the funnel when you decided to chase an answer. Otherwise, the chance that the witness escapes the deposition without providing complete answers to your questions will remain.

Closed Ended Questions

Q 6.3 What about closed ended questions?

Closed ended questions have the opposite goal of open ended ones. The closed ended question seeks affirmation of a single fact. Properly phrased, the closed ended question does not allow the witness to explain the answer given. The secret to the closed ended question resides in the language used.

Try to keep the closed ended question to six or seven words. Think in the language you learned when you began reading. Think of "See Spot run." The simple language makes for clarity in deposition questions. Simplicity avoids words with which the witness can quibble. The simple form of question also avoids adverbs and adjectives that seek to characterize the basic fact contained in the question.

You can add characterizations to a basic fact after the witness agrees with the basic fact. Trying to make the characterization first may allow the witness to avoid conceding the underlying fact. For example, let's say it was important to your case that the witness belonged to a very exclusive country club. You might phrase the question like this: "Sir, you belong to a very exclusive country club?" This question goes right to the point. The witness might agree, and if so, you are done with this line of questioning. But the witness might also disagree that the club is "very exclusive." If so, you have to build up to the conclusion by using one fact at a time. You could try an approach like this:

Q. You belong to Green Acres Country Club?

Q. Green Acres Country Club has a waiting list for new members?

Q. Green Acres has a waiting list over three years for new members?

Q. You waited over two years to become a member of Green Acres?

Q. Green Acres Country Club has an initiation fee of $100,000 for new members?

Q. You paid $100,000 when you joined?

Q. Green Acres limits its membership to 250 active members?

Q. Green Acres has had the same membership limit since it was founded?

Q. To become a member of Green Acres you need the recommendation of a current member?

Q. You were recommended by a current member?

Q. The CEO of Fortune 100 Company belongs to Green Acres?

Q. The Managing Partner of the Tall Building Law Firm is a member?

Q. Sir, Green Acres is not open to everyone?

Q. Green Acres is exclusive in its membership selection?

Q. Green Acres is an exclusive club?

Q. Green Acres is a very exclusive club?

It takes a lot of questions to get to the final answer, but the technique should help you understand the importance of using the underlying facts to build to a conclusion. You could add or subtract from this list of questions. The level of detail will be dictated by the importance of the point to your case. And, in order to go to this level of detail, you would need enough preparation to know the details of Green Acres Country Club.

The clever questioner will also now recognize that you could have gathered a lot of this information during the discovery phase of the deposition by using a funnel focused on Green Acres Country Club's membership process and criteria. The witness might even use some language in answering those questions that will help you rephrase your questions. If he called the process "selective," you would look for ways to use selective process in the questions above.

Rephrasing Questions

Q 6.3.1 What if I asked the closed ended question with too many qualifiers and didn't get the answer I sought?

Restart the process with a question that has no qualifiers. Then add one qualifier at a time to see which one is causing the witness to avoid your answer. Alternatively, ask the witness to tell you why they could not agree with your question. Remember, this is a discovery deposition, there is no downside to asking the why question.

There could be a downside to asking a why question in a deposition taken of a third party who is not likely to appear live at trial. In that situation, the why question may allow evidence to come into the record that the other side would not have thought to seek on their own. So, for the witness that is not likely to be at trial, you might want to be more careful regarding why questions.

Encouraging a Witness to Talk

Q 6.4 Are there other ways to get useful information in a deposition?

Yes. A truthful lawyer will admit that the best testimony in depositions often comes from uninvited comments by the witness on areas that were not in their outline.

Q 6.4.1 How do you get a witness to make such unsolicited statements?

You have to create an environment that encourages the witness to talk beyond the question you have asked. In other words, you want the witness to violate the rules given during the witness preparation process. *See* chapter 10. The witness will need to feel that his extra comments are welcomed and that he or she is being helpful by continuing to talk.

Your attitude has to be friendly. Witnesses will not volunteer information to you if you are rude or aggressive. You should not move to strike information that a witness gives that goes beyond your question. Listen to what the witness says and decide if you need to re-ask your question again to get a narrower response. But when you re-ask the question, do not show any signs of irritation with the witness. In fact, you may want to thank the witness for the additional information and suggest that you will follow up on that point in just a minute, but then ask him or her to answer the specific question you asked.

Q 6.4.2 What else can I do to get the witness to talk?

In a normal conversation, we all respond to non-verbal cues that we pick up from the other person in the conversation. We also fear a prolonged period of silence. You can use these techniques to aid your questioning style. How? Don't be afraid to look at the witness and just silently wait to see if the witness has more to say on a question. Silence can be your friend. The witness may decide he or she needs to fill the silence. Look at the witness in a way that suggests you are expecting more from him or her in answer to your question. Use a hand gesture to suggest that the witness should keep talking. A witness may respond to any or all of these techniques.

Notes to Chapter 6

1. Of course, a different answer might require you to use the police report with the witness to establish the police report as being the official report completed by the officers on the scene concerning the accident that day.

2. Any sudden recall of events that seeks to contradict the recollection of the events by the plaintiff and Mr. Bystander will subject the defendant to a cross-examination directed to his sudden, convenient recovery of his memory.

3. Note that in this example, when the lawyer uses the defendant perspective for the questions, the lawyer refers to the collision as an accident. Why? So that the questions suggest that the collision was unavoidable.

7

The Deposition of a Corporate Entity

Business entities frequently have information relevant to a case. In the "old" days, uncovering this information required the depositions of the entity's employees. Sometimes that deposition process would not provide answers because no single employee had the answer. Even before imposing deposition limits, the procedural rule makers decided that the entity itself could be subjected to a deposition. Often called a 30(b)(6) deposition after the federal rule allowing for such depositions, the business entity deposition has become a very effective way of gaining the entity's knowledge.

Deposing an entire entity poses special challenges and creates significant opportunities. The well-schooled litigator will make frequent use of this technique.

Reasons to Depose an Entity

Q 7.1 Why would you ever depose a corporate entity?

The ability to depose a corporation is one of the greatest discovery weapons available under the rules. By deposing the corporate entity, you remove the ability of individual witnesses to claim a lack of knowledge of various parts of the corporation's knowledge. And, even if witnesses are answering questions as truthfully as possible, there may be some knowledge that is only held collectively by the corporation through the knowledge of multiple employees. Finally, the organization, as long as it is a party, may be questioned about its opinions, including the contentions it has asserted in the litigation.[1] The deposing party also has a ready-made sanctions motion should the corporate party not prepare its representative properly to testify on the designated topics. As a result, the corporate deposition notice puts a lot of pressure on the corporate defendant.

Q 7.1.1 How did a corporate deposition come about?

When the Federal Rules of Civil Procedure added the rule allowing the deposition of a corporation in 1970, the purpose of the rule was to streamline the deposition process. Under the prior process, the deposing party would name an individual to be deposed and then seek to hold that person to be a "managing agent" of the entity such that his testimony would be binding on the entity. The rule also sought to "curb the 'bandying' by which officers or managing agents of a corporation are deposed in turn but each disclaims knowledge of facts that are clearly known to persons in the organization and thereby to it."[2] For the entity, the rule was designed to reduce the number of its employees that were deposed by a party that was uncertain as to who had the relevant knowledge.[3] Courts had held that the corporation had no burden to determine the person who should testify on its behalf.[4]

Q 7.1.2 Are corporate depositions available in both federal and state cases?

Yes. Some form of corporate representative deposition is now available in every jurisdiction. *See* Appendix A.

Rules Governing an Entity Deposition

Q 7.2 What are the rules for a corporate deposition?

Let's use Rule 30(b)(6) as our model:

> In its notice or subpoena, a party may name as the deponent a public or private corporation, a partnership, an association, a governmental agency, or other entity and must describe with reasonable particularity the matters for examination. The named organization must then designate one or more officers, directors, or managing agents, or designate other persons who consent to testify on its behalf; and it may set out the matters on which each person designated will testify. A subpoena must advise a nonparty organization of its duty to make this designation. The persons designated must testify about information known or reasonably available to the organization. This paragraph (6) does not preclude a deposition by any other procedure allowed by these rules.[5]

The rule requires a notice to be issued which names the organizational entity to be deposed. Rule 30(b)(6) lists corporations, partnerships, associations, and governmental agencies, but then concludes with the catch-all phrase making it applicable to "other entities." The rule is designed to cover any form of business entity.

The notice must also describe with "reasonable particularity" the matters that are to be the subject of the deposition. What is reasonable particularity? The best answer is that the matters must be described in such a way that the deponent entity can identify the "outer limits" of the proposed questioning.[6] Clarity is important in framing the matters for the deposition, but the deponent also has an obligation to seek to clarify the category descriptions should there be any ambiguity.

The named entity then has the obligation to designate one or more people to testify on its behalf. A lot of people believe that the obligation is to designate the most qualified person to testify on a topic. The rule contains no such obligation. The rule simply requires that the designee be an officer, director, managing agent, or another person who consents to testify on behalf of the entity. Note that the other person does not have to be an employee of the entity. This person must simply consent to testifying on the entity's behalf. The entity may also name multiple people to testify in response to a 30(b)(6) notice.

The entity must, however, designate the witness and the areas they will cover prior to the deposition. And, the entity has the responsibility to ensure that the selected witness is properly prepared. That obligation extends to all "information known or reasonably available to the organization."

Q 7.2.1 How far does the organization have to go to prepare its witnesses?

The answer is very far indeed. The obligation to prepare goes well beyond the personal knowledge of the witness. It includes the knowledge of the entity and that knowledge that is reasonably known to it. "Corporations, partnerships, and joint ventures have a duty to make a conscientious, good-faith effort to designate knowledgeable persons for Rule 30(b)(6) depositions and to prepare them to fully and unevasively answer questions about the designated subject matter."[7] The entity may have to have its witness review deposition transcripts, exhibits, and other documents.[8] If the entity lacks the information needed to prepare its witness, the entity must engage in a good faith effort to find that information. The entity may be required to reach out to former employees, agents, or other third parties, for example. The entity cannot compel its former employees or third parties to cooperate with its request for additional information, but it has the obligation to ask.

The witness can also rely on information provided to him by the entity's lawyers, either inside or outside counsel. While this might save time, it is not a recommended practice since the lawyer may waive work product protections by providing the information directly to the witness. Remember that the witness will be asked to disclose all steps taken to prepare for the deposition and would have to disclose his conversations with lawyers that provided him with information used to prepare his answers.

Q 7.2.2 Must the 30(b)(6) witness be the "most knowledgeable" witness on a particular topic?

No. The rule does not contain any such language. The witness must be knowledgeable at the time of the deposition, but there is no requirement that the witness have any pre-existing knowledge. The possibility of endless fights over which witness has the most knowledge of a given topic can be avoided.

The flip side protection given to the party taking the 30(b)(6) deposition is that the entity is bound to the answers provided by the witness. As a result, the entity will want to make sure that its witness answers the questions well.

Q 7.2.3 Are there any limits on the obligation to prepare the witness?

There are several possible limitations, but none that can be relied upon with any degree of certainty. The 2016 Amendments to the Federal Rules of Civil Procedure enhanced the concept that discovery efforts need to be "proportional to the needs of the case."[9] There is some level of preparation that would exceed the bounds of proportionality. But, it is likely that the level of effort would be viewed by a judge as the same as the "reasonable effort" standard imposed under Rule 30(b)(6).

Q 7.2.4 Are the obligations to prepare a witness any different for a non-party entity?

Maybe. The deposition of the non-party is governed by the subpoena rules. Under Rule 45, an obligation is imposed on the party issuing the subpoena to "take reasonable steps to avoid imposing undue burden or expense."[10] This language shifts the burden slightly from the deposed entity to the deposing party. And, the analysis under the reasonable proportionality standard should be different when applied to a third party.

Problems Facing an Entity Deposition

Q 7.3 What are the practical issues facing the party issuing a 30(b)(6) notice?

Formulation of the exact language of the subject matters to be covered in the deposition becomes critical. Think of the language of the subject matters in the notice as if it was a contract. The language used will define the obligation of the entity to prepare its witnesses.

Secondly, there are no limitations on the number of categories that can be included in a 30(b)(6) deposition notice. But, there is a seven-hour time limitation for each designated person absent agreement or court order. And, many courts now impose a total number of hours limitation on all depositions taken by a side in a case.

Q 7.3.1 What are the types of areas to cover in a 30(b)(6)?

There is no rule governing topic selection. Generally, the 30(b)(6) deposition is used as a quick way to discover the entity's knowledge relating to the matters in suit. These types of depositions help find answers to document maintenance and production questions and can be useful to identify the individuals within the entity that need to be separately deposed. The 30(b)(6) deposition can also be useful to find out the opinions and contentions of an entity that is a party to the litigation.

Q 7.3.2 When should a 30(b)(6) deposition be conducted?

Again, there is no rule requiring 30(b)(6) depositions to proceed in any given order. Many lawyers will begin discovery with the 30(b)(6) deposition in order to discover the way in which the entity is structured, who the key players are, what types of document systems are employed, and what types of reports are done on a regular basis. These lawyers will use the 30(b)(6) process as a way to map out the rest of their case discovery efforts.

Other lawyers will wait until after some individual depositions have been taken or responses to initial written discovery have been received before taking a 30(b)(6) deposition. These lawyers believe they need some exposure to the entity's operations in order to frame their subject matter requests more clearly.

But, if you do not know the names of any individuals, the 30(b)(6) route is the way to go. The entity will provide you with all the information you need to conduct the rest of your discovery.

Responding to an Entity Deposition Notice

Q 7.4 What does the designated entity need to do when it receives a 30(b)(6) notice?

Task number one is to review the language of the subject matter requests carefully. Make sure you understand what you are being asked to testify about. Any doubts should be resolved prior to the deposition. Courts will not look kindly on an entity that interprets a designated subject unilaterally without discussions with the requesting party to resolve any ambiguity.

Task number two is to prepare a formal response to the notice. That response must be very clear on areas where testimony will be provided, and it must object to topics that are overly broad, burdensome, or lack proportionality. But, the objection must specify the reasons the request is objectionable. Merely raising an objection without providing the underlying rationale for the objection is no longer enough. For example, if the objection is based on the burden imposed on the entity to collect the information, the objection must explain the details of the effort required to collect the information. If there is another set of information that is not as burdensome to search but provides the same, or close to the same, information, then the response should indicate that the witness will discuss that information instead. The guiding principle in the objections should be to give a clear understanding to the noticing party of the topics on which the witness will testify and the topics on which no witness will be proffered based on an objection.

Q 7.5 Must the responding party identify its witness or witnesses in advance of the deposition?

Yes. The rule requires that the witness be designated. Sometimes the responding party will not know the name of its designee when the response to the notice is due. If so, inform the other side in writing before the scheduled deposition day—the farther in advance the better. Remember that multiple witnesses may have to respond to the non-objectionable topics in the notice. In that case, you must provide the names of all witnesses and the specific topics that each will address.

Q 7.5.1 What if it takes more than one witness to cover a topic?

If you need two witnesses to handle a single topic, your designation should lay out the boundaries of where the witnesses will testify. But, understand there is a high likelihood that each witness will be asked to comment on the areas within the topic allocated to the other witness. We will talk about how to prepare the 30(b)(6) witness in the next section.

A possible approach to avoid the two witnesses covering the same ground is to offer both witnesses for simultaneous testimony. The concept requires the agreement of the noticing party, but allows both witnesses, or more witnesses, to address a topic or to add information to the testimony of another witness. The advantage is that it saves both parties litigation costs. The downside may be that the witnesses will disagree on answers to questions. But, that disagreement would likely have arisen in separate depositions and, in the committee deposition, the witnesses may talk to one another to clarify the issue on the spot. The concept is rarely used, but might make sense sometimes.[11]

Q 7.5.2 Should the responding party file for a protective order?

The answer to this question depends on several issues. The biggest question may be the percentage of categories to which the responding party has objected—the higher the percentage of categories with objections, the greater the likelihood that the other side will seek court intervention. And, if a judicial fight is inevitable, the responding party may want to explain its positions in the first filing.

Selecting an Entity Deposition Representative

Q 7.6 How do you select the 30(b)(6) designee?

The rules do not require you to select the most knowledgeable witness to testify on behalf of the entity. However, most entities will select an individual with some pre-existing knowledge of the topics specified in the notice. Why? Because that pre-existing knowledge will reduce the time required to make sure the witness is prepared to answer the questions.

But, there are other considerations that should come into play as well. For example, how will the witness under consideration perform as a deposition witness? Will he or she listen to the question and answer the question that is asked? Is he or she likely to volunteer information? Will the witness come across as a good representative of the entity? Remember that the video of the deposition might be shown in court some day.

How willing is the witness to give the time to prepare for and then sit through the deposition? What will be the cost to the entity of having the witness devote the time required? Is the witness someone already on the other side's deposition radar? Can you save the witness until trial? What role has the witness played in the trial preparation process? What other areas outside of the notice are within the witness's knowledge? Are these additional areas ones that you would like to keep out of discovery?

Many similar questions can be asked. The end goal is to have a witness that has the time for preparation and the presence to be well received should the video of his or her testimony ever be played in court. Work with the entity to identify the possible candidates and then interview them before you make your final selections.

Preparing an Entity Deposition Witness

Q 7.7 How do you prepare a 30(b)(6) witness?

Once you have looked at the topics, decided on your objections, and selected your witness or witnesses, the hard work begins. From the lawyer's perspective, the next task is to view the topics through the lens of the noticing party. Knowing what you know about the case, start a list of deposition questions you would ask your client related to the case. You will use these questions to ensure that your witness is properly prepared.

Task two is to locate the documents that relate to the topics. Look both in the document production database and other locations within the entity. You may discover a gap in your document production. If so, fix the gap before the deposition. Hopefully your prior document production efforts have been complete, but the 30(b)(6) witness will be asked about documents and databases with information so you would be well advised to double check the document production completeness as well. The documents you collect will help your designated witness in preparing for the deposition.

Task three requires scheduling enough time with your witness to prepare prior to the deposition. At least two sessions spaced apart by a few days is recommended. Why? Witnesses do not do all the homework necessary to be prepared to testify without lots of follow up. You will have to assign homework and be prepared to follow up with the witness to make sure the homework is completed. You will have to arrange some interviews for the witness to round out their knowledge. But, be careful about being the only source for information held by the witness. Always provide the witness with another source of the information you convey to maintain the privilege for your communications.

Multiple meetings with the witness are the only way to ensure that the witness is preparing to testify. At each meeting you can test the witness's knowledge level and make suggestions for areas where additional knowledge is required. Then, in the final meeting right before the deposition, you can focus on preparing the witness on how to testify on deposition day.

Q 7.7.1 Are there limits on witness preparation?

Yes, there is a practical limitation you need to remember. Do not have the witness learn new information outside the scope of the 30(b)(6) topics for which the witness has been designated. You do not want to increase the witness's knowledge beyond the topics for which they are designated because the testimony the witness provides will be considered that of the entity.

Q 7.7.2 What if the witness already has some knowledge on 30(b)(6) topics for which they are not the designated witness?

In the preparation process, you will want to show the witness the 30(b)(6) topics to see on what other areas they may have some knowledge. If they express knowledge in other areas, you must determine whether they are the right witness to cover that topic or whether another witness would do better. Assuming you decide that another witness would be better, you must make sure that the witness agrees with your assessment.

Agreement may be based on any number of points. Perhaps the witness agrees that you have selected another witness with the most pre-existing knowledge. But, the witness will almost always agree if you explain the additional time and effort it will take for that witness to be prepared to be the entity's witness on other topics.

Once you have obtained the witness's agreement, you must also prepare the witness on how to respond to questions in the area where they have some knowledge. Even though the witness is not designated in the area, you have to assume that the other side will uncover the witness's likely knowledge as they explore their history with the entity.

Technically, you may object to questions directed to topics outside of the witness's designated areas. And, for purposes of the record, you should make such objections because you may have different testimony from the designated witness on that topic and you will want the designated witness's testimony to bind the entity.

Your objection is not likely to stop the questions from proceeding. Most courts will only allow you to instruct the witness not to answer a question on grounds of privilege. Privilege would not apply to this situation. But, you can prepare your witness to say he has not prepared to testify on that topic on behalf of the entity. Then, the witness can say that in his individual capacity the answer is whatever he thinks the answer might be. If your witness is not capable of making these statements on his own, then you should note after you make an objection that the witness may answer the question in his individual capacity.

This approach at least clarifies that the witness is not providing testimony binding on the entity. True, you may have to deal with inconsistent answers between your witnesses. But, that situation is likely to arise in any case with multiple witnesses, and by following this approach, you make sure that the entity is bound only by the testimony of the witness you have chosen for a topic.

Q 7.7.3 Any other advice for preparing the 30(b)(6) witness?

Yes. Because the likelihood of motion practice around the preparation of the 30(b)(6) witness is high, create detailed records of the predeposition effort the witness undertook. Include in your notes the other people to whom the witness spoke and the documents he or she reviewed. You will want your witness to keep some notes of who he or she spoke to and what he or she reviewed, but remember that the notes made by the witness may be discoverable during the deposition.

Keeping such records as your witness prepares will also help you gauge whether a court will later determine the preparation efforts to be reasonable. You will use your notes to help the witness prepare an affidavit of his preparation activities in response to any motion.

Binding Nature of Entity Testimony

Q 7.8 How binding is the testimony of a 30(b)(6) witness on the entity?

Interestingly, the rule makes no comment about the degree to which testimony from a designated witness binds the entity. Courts, however, agree that the testimony is binding. The debate occurs over the degree to which the testimony of the designated witness binds the entity.

Some courts take the view that the 30(b)(6) testimony is an admission by the entity. During the deposition, "there is no distinction between the corporate representative and the corporation."[12] These admissions bind the corporation, unless there is good reason to permit the entity to be excused from its admission. In *Hyde v. Stanley Tools*,[13] for example, the court looked to see if new information had become available since the deposition that the entity could not have had prior to the deposition. Failing to find such evidence, the court did not allow a later deposition to alter the prior 30(b)(6) testimony.

The majority view treats the 30(b)(6) testimony just as it would any other deposition testimony. According to these courts, the testimony of a 30(b)(6) designee is not "absolutely binding" on the entity.[14] But, even these courts require a reasonable explanation as to why the new testimony was not offered as part of the 30(b)(6) deposition.

As a practical matter, assume that the testimony of the 30(b)(6) witness will bind the entity and prepare the witness accordingly. If the designated witness does not know the answer to a key question, the entity may be precluded from later introducing evidence on the topic.

Q 7.9 Can you revise "bad" 30(b)(6) testimony?

Yes. The entity has the same right to read and review the transcript prior to it becoming final as do all witnesses. Substantive changes to the testimony, however, are subject to comment at trial—better to allow such comments to be made than to allow inaccurate testimony to stand.

You might also be able to use Rule 26(e)(2) to supplement or correct the 30(b)(6) testimony. Rule 26(e) addresses changing responses to interrogatories, requests for production, and requests for admission. Rule 30(b)(6) depositions are not mentioned, but at least one court has allowed use of the rule because a Rule 30(b)(6) deposition is designed to obtain an entity's positons.[15] If available, Rule 26(e) allows a correction to be made in a timely manner after the entity discovers that a prior response is "incomplete or incorrect."

Notes to Chapter 7

1. The corporate party would not be required to testify about litigation positions that are the result of attorney opinion work product. *See* Albert v. DRS RSTA, Inc., No. 6-11-cv- 869-ORL (M.D. Fla. Aug. 17, 2012).

2. Notes of Advisory Committee on Rules—1970 Amendment Comment to Rule 30(b)(6) (citing Haney v. Woodward & Lothrop, Inc., 330 F.2d 940, 944 (4th Cir. 1964)).

3. The concept of imposing limitations on the number or length of depositions had not yet become acceptable.

4. *E.g.*, United States v. Gahagan Dredging Corp., 24 F.R.D. 328, 329 (S.D.N.Y. 1958). A good summary of the law on corporate depositions at the federal level can be found in QBE Ins. Corp. v. Jorda Enters., Inc., 277 F.R.D. 676 (S.D. Fla. 2012).

5. FED. R. CIV. P. 30(b)(6).

6. *See, e.g.*, Reed v. Bennett, 193 F.R.D. 689 (D. Kan. 2000); Tri-State Hosp. Supply Corp. v. United States, 226 F.R.D. 118 (D.D.C. 2005).

7. Starlight Int'l, Inc. v. Herlihy, 186 F.R.D. 626, 639 (D. Kan. 1999), citing Dravo Corp. v. Liberty Mut. Ins. Co., 164 F.R.D. 70, 75 (D. Neb. 1995).

8. *See* United States v. Taylor, 166 F.R.D. 356, 361 (M.D.N.C. 1996).

9. FED. R. CIV. P. 26(b)(1).

10. FED. R. CIV. P. 45(d)(1).

11. The concept is explained in more detail in an article by Jerold Solovy and Robert Byman, "Deposition by Committee." The article may be found at: https://jenner.com/system/assets/assets/4557/original/05_17_2004_Deposition_By_Committee.pdf?13201.

12. Hyde v. Stanley Tools, 107 F. Supp. 2d 992, 992–93 (E.D. La. 2000), *aff'd*, 31 F. App'x 151 (5th Cir. 2001).

13. *Id.*

14. State Farm Mut. Auto. Ins. Co. v. New Horizont, Inc., 250 F.R.D. 203, 212 (E.D. Pa. 2008) (quoting 8A CHARLES ALAN WRIGHT, FEDERAL PRACTICE AND PROCEDURE § 2103 (Supp. 2007).

15. *See* Diamond Triumph Auto Glass, Inc. v. Safelite Glass Corp., 441 F. Supp. 2d 695, 723 n.17 (M.D. Pa. 2006).

8

Expert Witness Depositions

Deposing an expert witness presents unique procedural and structural challenges. Most experts have experience in the deposition process and know how to advocate their expert position. Getting an expert to confess during a deposition that their positon is unfounded never happens.

Why, then, depose an expert? Most courts will require the expert to prepare a report disclosing the expert's opinions and the basis for those opinions. The report provides a roadmap of the expert's opinions, but the roadmap is often incomplete. A deposition can complete the map and expose areas where the expert has assumed a key answer that may contravene the evidence in the case. The deposition can also allow the exploration of biases that the expert may have and provide grounds for arguing that the expert should not be allowed to testify on all or part of his opinions. And, like all deposition witnesses, taking an expert's deposition allows you to judge the effectiveness of that witness at trial.

Expert Defined

Q 8.1 What is an expert?

An expert is a person with specialized knowledge gained by experience or training.[1] Rule 702 of the Federal Rules of Evidence defines an expert as:

> A witness who is qualified as an expert by knowledge, skill, experience, training, or education may testify in the form of an opinion or otherwise if:
>
> (a) the expert's scientific, technical, or other specialized knowledge will help the trier of fact to understand the evidence or to determine a fact in issue;
>
> (b) the testimony is based on sufficient facts or data;
>
> (c) the testimony is the product of reliable principles and methods; and
>
> (d) the expert has reliably applied the principles and methods to the facts of the case.

An expert can be anyone who has gained specialized knowledge relevant to an issue of a case. The trial court determines whether an expert may testify—a topic for another book. The point to remember is that not everyone with experience or training in a particular field can serve as an expert in a civil action. One key purpose of the expert deposition, besides the typical purposes of a deposition, is to determine whether the expert proposed by the other side should testify in your particular case. Cases can be won on successful motions to disqualify the expert for the other side. And, disqualification can be based on the expert's failure to meet the requirements of Rule 702.

Q 8.1.1 When may an expert testify?

Rule 702 permits an expert to testify if the expert's knowledge or experience will help the trier of fact to understand evidence or determine a fact in issue. The expert's opinion must be based on enough facts or data, be based on reliable principles and methods, and reflect the reliable application of the principles and methods to the facts of the case.

These requirements have been the subject of significant litigation. The Supreme Court makes trial judges the "gatekeeper" and imposes on them an obligation to keep unreliable expert testimony away from the jury.[2] Those cases, along with the requirements of Rule 702, provide a good starting outline for an expert deposition.

Q 8.1.2 On what may an expert rely?

Experts are not treated to the same evidentiary restrictions as lay witnesses. Experts need not observe the facts they use in their opinions. Experts may rely on information that any expert in their field would reasonably rely upon in forming an opinion on a subject. That information need not be independently admissible. Rule 703 of the Federal Rules of Evidence provides that "[a]n expert may base an opinion on facts or data in the case that the expert has been made aware of or personally observed. If experts in the particular field would reasonably rely on those kinds of facts or data in forming an opinion on the subject, they need not be admissible for the opinion to be admitted." The question becomes trying to understand what an expert in the field would normally do outside the litigation context. This area can be yet another fertile ground for deposition examination.

Preparing for the Expert Deposition

Q 8.2 What are the steps for preparing for an expert deposition?

Preparing for a regular witness deposition takes time, but an expert deposition requires much more. Experts have spent years developing their area of expertise. A lawyer cannot match that level of expertise before the day of the deposition. The lawyer can, however, master the facts of the case better than the expert.[3] The mastery of the facts provides an area in which the lawyer may have some success.

The lawyer must also gain some basic understanding of how the expert's area or expertise relates to the case. Hopefully, the expert on the taking lawyer's side will provide a primer of the area. Even with that help, the lawyer must take some time to gain a basic understanding to formulate questions that explore the opinions the expert is offering in the case. That area knowledge will also help identify the basic principles of the area of expertise to determine whether the expert has deviated from those principles. Identify the leading treatises, books, or scholarly articles in the area. Spend time reading those materials to further cement your understanding of the technical area. These scholarly materials may also provide sources for determining whether the expert opinions remain true to the scholarly materials. If not, additional areas of deposition questions may be formulated.

Q 8.2.1 How do you use the expert report to prepare?

Once the basic background has been examined, it is time to turn to the expert's report. You will return to the report several times prior to the deposition. On that first pass look to see if the report complies with the requirements of Federal Rule of Civil Procedure 26. Under that rule, the expert report must contain:

(i) a complete statement of all opinions the witness will express and the basis and reasons for them;

(ii) the facts or data considered by the witness in forming them;

(iii) any exhibits that will be used to summarize or support them;

(iv) the witness's qualifications, including a list of all publications authored in the previous 10 years;

(v) a list of all other cases in which, during the previous 4 years, the witness testified as an expert at trial or by deposition; and

(vi) a statement of the compensation to be paid for the study and testimony in the case.[4]

Each category also provides areas of potential questions for the expert.

Before turning to formulating deposition questions, scour the report to see what it says in response to each category. The goal is to prepare an outline of the report that will allow you to examine its contents and its reasoning. The outline will be useful for the actual deposition. Make note of each opinion in the report and separately list each reason that the expert articulates to support their conclusions. Then, search carefully for the facts or assumptions that underlie those rationales and add them to the outline. Include any exhibits or deposition testimony that the expert cites.

When the outline is complete, it is time to make notations of areas where the facts conflict with the expert's stated facts or assumptions. Double check the basis of the facts on which you are relying. If you challenge the expert's factual assumptions, you want to be correct.

Next, make special note of all areas where you agree with the expert. Every fact, rationale, or opinion on which there is agreement can bolster your side of the case. These areas of agreement will be items to nail down during the deposition.

In your review of the areas of disagreement and agreement, you are seeking to identify the issue that separates the expert from your expert. Is there a different application of some fundamental premise in the area or expertise? Is the difference based on different assumptions? Has one expert reviewed more or different material from the other? By figuring out the difference, you can explain why your expert has the correct answer and the other expert does not.

Finally, look for word choices that suggest the expert has become an advocate for his side of the case. Adverbs and adjectives are key words to examine in this process. The expert that overstates a point or exaggerates a fact will be easier to discredit at trial. The jury will see that the expert has become an advocate for the party that hired him as opposed to an independent expert. The expert's behavior will feed the jury's natural suspicion of the hired expert.[5] During the deposition, the goal is to lock the expert into the exaggerations or overstatements. But, even if they walk back from the language of the report, you may have developed an area that can be used at trial.

Q 8.2.2 How can your expert help you get ready?

Besides providing a subject tutorial, your expert can help with deciphering the report and preparing deposition questions. The secret to dealing with your expert is to understand what suggested areas are potentially useful to the case and what proposed questions are so technical they will only distract from the case. Experts sometimes get caught up in the game of proving that they are the better expert. This is a game that no one else in the lawsuit plays. The answers that result from those highly technical questions will not prove useful, but they will consume precious time from the deposition.

Nonetheless, your expert will also provide you with several questions that demonstrate the fundamental difference between the opinions of the experts. These questions are important. But, to understand those questions and the purpose of asking them, you must have several conversations with your expert. During those discussions, ask the purpose behind each proposed question. That question will provoke more questions. The end result will be a better understanding of the questions you should ask and an increased understanding of the underlying subject matter. Asking questions suggested by your expert without understanding the purpose behind the questions will not lead to useful deposition testimony.

And, if there are not significant cost constraints, ask your expert to attend the deposition. Your expert's presence at the deposition should affect the expert. The expert will know that efforts to evade in the complicated language of the area of expertise will not be an option. The deposition may proceed more easily. Your expert is also likely to have new ideas for areas of questioning that arise from answers given by the expert.

Q 8.2.3 How can the other side's expert help you prepare?

The expert you are about to depose likely has a long track record. Search that record looking for items that will help your case. Again, depending upon cost restraints, your expert can help with this review. You will also want to look for prior cases in which the expert filed a report and/or testified, at trial or deposition. Collect that prior testimony and reports. Some of that prior testimony may be under a protective order, but seek as much as is available.[6]

As you look through these materials, you are looking for times where the expert offered different views on the matter in your case. Those differences may focus on views of the area of expertise or may involve the fundamental opinions of the expert. Some experts will shape their testimony to aide a particular case. Some experts will stretch the area of the expertise to support a particular case. That shaping of testimony or stretching of opinions can be used against the expert in your case and will be items to add to your deposition outline.

Last, you will want to check for judicial decisions referring to the expert. Whether the expert's views have been subjected to prior judicial scrutiny can help formulate a plan to attack the expert's opinion in your case. If a court has disavowed the theory, the plan of attack is simple. Look for the rationale used by the court to exclude the opinion and confirm that the same approach and infirmity(ies) exist in the report.

Do not be surprised that the expert has not changed his methodology. The expert may not have had time to make the change or the expert may believe that the court analysis is wrong. There may also be an appeal of the prior court's ruling. Whatever the reason, use the prior opinion to your advantage.

Even if a court has affirmed the expert's approach, the opinion doing so may provide useful information for you. Read the opinion carefully to see if the court was troubled by any part of the expert's opinions or the approach used to support the opinions. Judges will often identify areas on which they could not exclude the expert's opinions but which will make great cross-examination material.

Questioning the Expert

Q 8.3 Is the expert deposition different from a lay witness?

Yes. Experts are very experienced in the deposition process. That experience allows them to avoid answering questions they find to be problematic. Even experts without deposition experience can hide in the technical speak of their area of expertise. And, all experts will look for an opportunity to repeat their conclusions often in response to any question asked.

To address these expert tactics, you must pay extra attention to the form of your question, display a command of the situation (even if you only fake that command), and be determined to stick to your deposition goal. Experts look for the inexperienced lawyer lacking the skills to push them to answer the question asked.

Q 8.3.1 What's different about the form of the question?

The same general forms of questions are available: open ended or closed ended. The technique with the expert requires a greater focus on the language used in those questions. There will be times to ask open ended questions and times to ask closed ended questions. Special care must be given to the questions asked. Given the expert's desire to avoid answering questions discussed above, all questions must be shortened to exclude, as much as possible, extra words that will give the expert an opportunity to evade an answer.

Learning to exclude extra words from the question is a skill best developed by practice. As you ask questions, watch how the witness responds. Figure out what was in your question that permitted the expert to avoid answering it. As you engage in that examination, ask the question again with fewer words. This process repeated over time will help you improve.

The key to asking the short question of the expert is making sure you know what it is you are trying to extract from the expert. Keep it simple and direct. For example, you will want to know the information that the expert relied upon in formulating the opinions being offered.

So, ask the expert a question like, "Tell me what you relied upon in forming your opinion?" Remember the funnel technique and ask the repeat question "What else?" until the answer is "there is no more." As with any application of the funnel technique, ask questions that also suggest information you think, based on conversations with your expert, the expert should have reviewed in forming an opinion.

Q 8.3.2 What areas should be covered with the expert?

The expert presents several potential areas for examination. The secret is to select the areas that will be most productive. Some areas to consider as you make your deposition outline are:

1. *Sources and Content of Information Reviewed.* Establishing an exhaustive list of the items, conversations, and other materials reviewed by the expert might be the number one objective of the expert deposition. The report will contain a listing of the items relied upon by the expert in formulating their opinion. Some experts will not include items they reviewed, but did not rely upon in formulating their opinion.[7] Hence, there is a need to use the deposition to explore any gap in information disclosed. The purpose of creating an exhaustive list of information reviewed, even if not relied upon, is to provide a basis to look for missing pieces of data that may undercut the opinion. The list may also provide additional sources of discovery or additional areas of information that your expert must review.

Include on the list conversations the expert might have had with counsel relating to their opinion. Many lawyers have the wrong assumption that conversations with the expert are privileged.[8] Under Rules 26(b)(4)(B) and (C), only some portion of those conversations remain protected:

> (B) Trial-Preparation Protection for Draft Reports or Disclosures. Rules 26(b)(3)(A) and (B) protect drafts of any report or disclosure required under Rule 26(a)(2), regardless of the form in which the draft is recorded.
>
> (C) Trial-Preparation Protection for Communications Between a Party's Attorney and Expert Witnesses. Rules 26(b)(3)(A) and (B) protect communications between the party's attorney and any

> witness required to provide a report under Rule 26(a)(2)(B), regardless of the form of the communications, *except to the extent that the communications*:
>
> (i) *relate to compensation for the expert's study or testimony;*
>
> (ii) *identify facts or data that the party's attorney provided and that the expert considered in forming the opinions to be expressed; or*
>
> (iii) *identify assumptions that the party's attorney provided and that the expert relied on in forming the opinions to be expressed.*

(italics added). Each of the three listed exceptions should be on the list of questions for the expert.

2. *Sources of Information Not Reviewed or Tests or Investigations Not Performed.* As a practical matter, experts always have a dream list of items to review, tests to perform, analysis to conduct, or people to interview. The problem is that each of those additional items costs money and parties often have cost constraints that limit the expert's ability to conduct a complete examination. And, experts are nervous about information that was not available to them or analysis not performed. Experts fear that the one item left unexplored may provide a basis to undermine their opinion. Here is an area where the expert is not on superior footing to the questioner. Spend enough time on the topic to make sure there are no additional items on the expert's wish list that have not been disclosed. Then, in consultation with your expert, decide which area will provide the best avenue of attack in a *Daubert* motion or at trial.

3. *Where Appropriate, Ask the Questions Suggested by* Daubert. The Supreme Court laid out several considerations for district courts as they exercise their "gatekeeper" function. Generally, the Court laid out three requirements: (1) the expert must be qualified; (2) the testimony must be relevant; and (3) the testimony must be reliable.[9] Each area provides a potential basis for questioning.

If the expert's qualifications to offer the opinion given are not obvious from the information provided in the report, appropriate questions will arise. One question that may shorten that process is to have the expert tell you why his education, knowledge, skill or experience qualifies him to give the opinion in the case.

Relevance is really a two-part inquiry—is the information helpful, and does it fit the facts of the case. The helpful inquiry is a fairly easy standard to meet and probably will not require much questioning. Whether the opinion fits the facts of the case, however, may prove to be a more fruitful area of inquiry. If the opinion rests on facts not supported by the undisputed facts in the case, the chances of excluding the expert increase exponentially.

The third area, reliability, provides the most productive area for deposition questions. In this area, the questions relate to the methods used or the principles applied by the expert in reaching their opinion. The principles and methods must provide evidence that the opinion is scientifically reliable. What that means for a particular case requires specific research as courts have developed specific requirements for different areas of expert testimony. Loosely stated, the inquiry is whether the expert used "reliable sources and provided reasoned explanations connecting the source material to his conclusion."[10]

The Supreme Court's *Daubert* opinion contained a "non-exhaustive" list of factors to consider in the reliability inquiry. The Court suggested looking to see if the expert theory is testable, if the opinion been subjected to peer review, what the known error rate to the methodology applied is, what standards, if any, apply, and the degree to which the expert's opinion is accepted by the scientific community.[11] Though the list sounds like it only applies to scientific experts, the Court was clear that the gatekeeper function applies to all areas of expert testimony.[12]

4. *Opinions Formed by the Expert.* The report contains opinions, but it may not contain all of the opinions formed by the expert. Some will suggest that asking for additional opinions provides the expert an opportunity to expand the report, and a court may allow the expert to testify to opinions not in the report but discussed during the deposition. Given that possibility, asking for opinions outside the report poses a risk. The risk might be acceptable in circumstances where the expert had other opinions that were not helpful to the final result. For example, a damages expert may have come to different conclusions on possible damages but only included one in the report. Early in the expert deposition experience, the risk of asking for other opinions may not be worth taking.

Q 8.3.3 How should you deal with the expert's superior technical knowledge?

The key is to remain confident in the questions you have asked. If the expert tries to hide his answers in complicated language of the expert's area of knowledge, you have a decision to make. It may be that the expert's language is so incomprehensible that you will want to use some of those answers before a jury. You may decide that the questions require answers to determine what the expert did, and to allow your expert to be prepared. If you make the choice to gain answers, be prepared to take the answer given and break it down to ask for explanations. Keep following that process until you, or your expert, are satisfied with the answer.

Notes to Chapter 8

1. *See* https://www.merriam-webster.com/dictionary/expert.

2. Daubert v. Merrell Dow Pharm., Inc., 509 U.S. 579 (1993), and Kumho Tire Co. v. Carmichael, 526 U.S. 137 (1999).

3. The mastery of the facts of the case covers a large ground. The lawyer must know the testimony of all witnesses and have command of the relevant documents produced by both sides. The lawyer must also know the relevant information from witnesses on their side of the cases that have not yet been deposed.

4. FED. R. CIV. P. 26(a)(2)(B).

5. *The Expert Witness Credibility Model: How Juries Perceive Expert Witnesses*, https://www.forensisgroup.com/the-expert-witness-credibility-model-how-juries-perceive-expert-witnesses/ (Apr. 2016).

6. One potential source of information is lawyers who have dealt with the expert in prior cases. Reach out to those lawyers to see what information they can share. They may have discovered some piece of information that will be of use in your case.

7. Federal Rule of Civil Procedure 26(2)(b)(ii) requires disclosure of "the facts or data considered by the witness in forming them." An expert may be exposed to a wide variety of information in the early stages of their investigation that do not lead them to form the opinions in the report.

8. When the Federal Rules were amended in 1993, the Committee Notes made clear that information given to a testifying expert would not be privileged. The Notes stated: *"The report is to disclose the data and other information considered by the expert and any exhibits or charts that summarize or support the expert's opinions. Given this obligation of disclosure, litigants should no longer be able to argue that materials furnished to their experts to be used in forming their opinions—whether or not ultimately relied upon by the expert—are privileged or otherwise protected from disclosure when such persons are testifying or being deposed."* In 2010, the rule was amended yet again to exclude communications related directly to draft expert reports from the obligation to disclose.

9. Daubert v. Merrell Dow Pharm., Inc., 509 U.S. 579 (1993).

10. Lees v. Carthage College, 714 F.3d 516, 524 (7th Cir. 2013).

11. *Daubert,* 509 U.S. at 593–94.

12. *See* Kumho Tire v. Carmichael, 536 U.S. 137, 150 (1999).

9

After the Deposition

The deposition is over. The last question has been asked. Both the taking lawyer and the defending lawyer exhale thinking their tasks are complete. Sadly, neither lawyer is correct. They both have significant tasks left before them. This chapter discusses those tasks, first for the taking lawyer and then for the defending lawyer.

The Taking Lawyer Tasks

Q 9.1 As the deposition concludes, why would the taking lawyer be having any further concerns?

The deposition was taken to achieve one or more specific purposes. Questions were not asked simply to say those questions had been asked. The questions were designed to discover information and to test theories. As the deposition concludes, assessing whether those purposes have been accomplished begins.

Q 9.1.1 How do you assess whether the purposes of the deposition have been accomplished?

Working from a rough transcript, start a list of the items learned from the deposition. Make a separate list of additional sources of potential information that the witness identified. Were additional sources of documents identified? If so, request those documents promptly. There may also be questions on whether those documents should have been produced sooner. Depending on the answer to that question, there may also be a motion for sanctions that needs to be considered.

Were new names identified by the witness as possible sources of information? If so, create a list of the newly identified individuals. Once you have the list, review the information to determine whether the newly identified individuals should also be deposed. Any one you decide to depose based on that identification must be noticed prior to the end of your discovery period. These additional depositions may put you over the court order discovery limits, which means you must also seek leave of court to conduct the additional discovery. And, as with the newly identified documents, you must assess whether the new names should have been disclosed earlier and, if so, whether a sanction motion is appropriate.

Q 9.1.2 What should you do with the testimony that was new information?

After determining whether additional discovery is necessary, turn to the areas where the deposition testimony affects the case. What did the witness say about key case elements? Does the witness's version of key events support your case or undermine the opposing side's interpretation? Or does the testimony undercut your side of the case? Is that testimony supported by other evidence, documents or testimony? How credible was the witness when discussing the evidence?

Remember that one main purpose of the deposition was to learn the other side's version of the case. Once you have heard the particular witness's version of events, critically assess that story, and you must do so objectively. Lawyers tend to identify with their side of the case. That tendency can lead to misanalysis of the facts and, more importantly, a misanalysis of the case as a whole. Proper assessment requires asking whether the witness's version of events could be believed by a reasonable finder of fact.

If the answer is yes, look for ways to challenge that story in future depositions. Also, determine if parts of the story are inconsistent with other evidence or are not logically consistent internally. Compile a list of the issues you find. You may well need to use these items to cross-examine the witness at trial.

Q 9.1.3 Does the testimony affect any case theories?

Assess the testimony to determine whether case theories were supported, contradicted, or untouched. Mark the testimony accordingly to make it easily available later. The task of marking testimony has become much easier in the various electronic deposition review software now available. Testimony can be flagged as relevant to a number of different categories and easily retrieved later.

Once marked, the assessment process must begin. Will the case theory survive the new testimony? How credible is the new testimony? Is that new testimony supported by additional evidence already discovered? Is there some basis to doubt the new testimony? How did the witness look when the testimony was given? Will the witness be subject to impeachment? Will the witness be subject to a bias attack that will discredit the testimony? Ask these and other questions that may occur to determine whether the case theory must be abandoned or otherwise altered.

If the testimony confirms or supports the case theory, the assessment process must still be carried out. Do not fall for the danger of ignoring signs that suggest weakness in the testimony supporting the case theory. By applying the same rigorous analysis, a true picture of the case theory's strengths and weaknesses emerges. And, that resulting view provides a clear basis to value the underlying case.

Q 9.1.4 What role will the witness play later in the case?

Following the deposition of a witness is the best time to determine the role the witness will likely play in the case. Will the witness be a major witness providing key testimony for one side or the other? Will the witness provide corroboration for a major witness? Or, will the witness play no role in the case? Answering these questions guides the level of effort required to prepare for that witness at trial. As you suspect, the more important the witness is likely to be the greater the effort to prepare for that witness at trial.

The Defending Lawyer Tasks

Q 9.2 What should the defending lawyer focus on after the deposition?

The first concern of the defending lawyer is the witness. After the deposition is completed, the defending lawyer should spend time with the witness discussing the deposition. The witness will want an assessment of their performance. Be careful of the answer to this question. At the end of the deposition, the witness will be physically and emotionally exhausted. The witness need not hear every mistake they made in responding to questions. Instead, leave the witness with a positive feeling. But, make notes of areas to work on should the witness testify again.

And, the completion of the deposition may be the first time the defending lawyer has had a chance to discuss the witness's testimony since the deposition began, as many jurisdictions prohibit the defending lawyer from discussing the substance of the witness's testimony once the deposition began. *See* chapter 2 and Appendix A. The witness will likely have several substantive questions that need to be addressed. The defending lawyer may also have follow-up questions to learn more about any new areas that arose during the deposition. In particular, the witness may have identified new sources of documents and/or additional document locations. The end of the deposition is the time to raise these items with the witness because the taking lawyer will be following up the next day. Learn all you can about these new witnesses and documents and determine if the witness can assist in contacting witnesses or locating documents.

Q 9.2.1 What if the witness raised new facts during the deposition?

No matter how much preparation prior to the deposition, the witness may identify new facts for the first time in the deposition. The defending lawyer must determine whether those "new" facts are important to the case. The witness should also be pressed to determine the basis for the "new" facts. Are there documents to be collected and produced? Are there new witnesses that must be identified to the other side? Again, ask the witness these questions while the deposition remains fresh in their memory and make the appropriate plans to follow up.

And, just like the taking lawyer, the "new" facts must be evaluated critically. Are those facts supported by other witnesses or documents? Will the witness's rendition of those facts be credible? Is the case theme affected? The answer to these sorts of questions determines the changes that need to be made to the case plan. The case deposition preparation outline for other witnesses may need alteration, as well as the outline for questions of the other side's witnesses. Additional legal research may be required to determine the impact of the "new" facts on the case's legal theories.

Q 9.2.2 Are there issues for the witness after the deposition day ends?

Yes. The last phase of the deposition requires careful review of the official transcript when received from the court reporter, which will be delivered to the lawyer by the court reporter several days to a few weeks after the deposition is completed. Why? The official transcript is the version of the deposition used in all later court proceedings—summary judgment, other motions, hearings, and at trial. It is important that that the transcript is completely accurate. (Note that depending on the case budget, the lawyers may request real-time transcripts (simultaneous copies of the reporter's record or daily copies of the transcript) before the conclusion of the deposition. Such transcripts are to assist the lawyer with the witness and the case, but they are not the "official" transcript.)

Q 9.2.3 What do you look for as you review the transcript?

Several items should be examined. First, look for mistakes made by the court reporter. Was the question typed correctly? Was there something left out of an answer? Was there a typographical error that affects the meaning of the question or answer? These sorts of mistakes are rare. Court reporters as a group are very conscientious about their work, but they are human. If you identify transcription errors, ask the court reporter to recheck the audio recordings they made to see if they will acknowledge the mistake and correct it.

Second, look for areas where the witness's answers are incomplete, inaccurate, or need some amplification. Assuming the defending lawyer requested at the deposition to allow the witness to review and sign the transcript, a request that should almost always be made, the witness will have an ability to correct these items. Rule 30(e) of the Federal Rules of Civil Procedure provides a thirty-day period for the witness to review and sign a transcript.[1] The procedures allow the witness to change the "form or substance" of the transcript if a statement is attached that lists the changes and the reasons for making them. Providing reasons for the change allows the court to assess the reasonableness of the change. As a result, the more a change substantively alters the meaning of an answer, the more explanation for the reason behind the change that should be provided. Do not take this right as an opportunity to rewrite the deposition to improve its grammar or the word choices made by the witness unless necessary to do so. Both the original answer and the changed answer remain a part of the record.[2] Extensive changes may allow the other side to seek a reopening of the deposition to explore the changes made to the transcript. And, those changes, made after consultation with counsel, may be the subject of cross-examination at trial. The finder of fact may assess the credibility of the witness based on changes made to the transcript.

The lawyer must also resist the urge to change answers to reflect the way the lawyer would have preferred the question be answered. The deposition is not the testimony of the lawyer. The witness is the only person who took an oath, the violation of which is subject to perjury prosecution, and the testimony must remain that of the witness. The same rule applies to changes to a transcript. The lawyer should assist the witness with the review and correction, but the lawyer should not use that process to alter the witness's testimony.

Q 9.2.4 What procedure should be followed to review the transcript?

Rule 30(e) provides a thirty-day window to review the transcript and get any changes back to the court reporter. To use this time wisely, provide a copy of the transcript to the witness upon receipt from the court reporter and schedule a meeting or a conference call a week later to discuss the transcript with the witness. The scheduling of the call helps both the witness and the lawyer review the transcript timely. When the call occurs, the lawyer should focus on whether the changes the witness seeks to make are worth making. This decision is a judgment call, but generally the rule is to make no change unless doing so is required to make the answer given truthful or to clear up a major factual omission that the witness, upon reflection, believes is required to make the answer complete. If a change is to be made, discuss the reason for the change with the witness to complete the list of changes and reasons for those changes as required by Rule 30(e).

The lawyer may also suggest that certain changes be made. But do so only after discussing the matter with the witness and gaining the witness's agreement that the change the lawyer suggests results in a truthful answer. The lawyer must avoid the temptation to replace the witness's testimony with facts that the witness might later disavow.

Q 9.2.5 What happens after the review is completed?

The transcript should arrive with an errata sheet for making changes. Make sure that a complete list of any changes with the reason for the changes is completed. Review the changes with the witness one last time. If the witness agrees with all changes and explanations, have the witness sign the transcript the errata sheet, and have those signatures notarized.

Once you have the signed and notarized forms, deliver those documents to the court reporter. The court reporter will provide copies to the other side, but it is a good practice to send the other side a copy of any changes made to the transcript at the same time as it is sent to the court reporter.

Notes to Chapter 9

1. Rule 30(e) provides:

   Review by the Witness; Changes.

   (1) *Review; Statement of Changes.* On request by the deponent or a party before the deposition is completed, the deponent must be allowed 30 days after being notified by the officer that the transcript or recording is available in which:

      (A) to review the transcript or recording; and
      (B) if there are changes in form or substance, to sign a statement listing the changes and the reasons for making them.

   (2) *Changes Indicated in the Officer's Certificate.* The officer must note in the certificate prescribed by Rule 30(f)(1) whether a review was requested and, if so, must attach any changes the deponent makes during the 30-day period.

2. *See* Thorn v. Sundstrand Aerospace Corp., 207 F.3d 383 (7th Cir. 2000).

10

Preparing the Witness and Defending the Deposition

Until now, the focus of this book has been on the lawyer taking the deposition. That task is daunting, but the job of preparing the witness takes considerably greater effort. Witnesses come with various backgrounds and skills, but very few come with the knowledge and patience required to complete a deposition successfully. The defending lawyer must prepare the witness and then defend the deposition in such a way that allows the witness to succeed. What defines success? Every lawyer will likely have a different answer. Some will focus on the information provided to the other side. Others will evaluate whether the witness proved useful for the ultimate success of the case. And, yet others will simply focus on whether the deposition ended earlier than expected. From the witness's perspective, though, the answer is much simpler. The witness wants the deposition to end as quickly as possible with the minimum harm done to their side of the case. And third parties, with no interest in the case, seek only to have the deposition completed quickly.

Witness Preparation

Q 10.1 How do you know how much effort should go into witness preparation?

Every witness will be different. Each witness comes to the deposition process with a unique set of personality and life experiences that will be hard to alter in the deposition preparation process. And, trying to make drastic changes to a witness's normal way of communicating will likely create hostility since witnesses do not appreciate efforts to change the skills and personality traits that have proven useful to them in life.

Before a lawyer can decide the effort required, the lawyer must spend time evaluating the witness. Determine the witness's natural manner of responding to questions by asking questions about their understanding of the issues involved in the case. Listen carefully to how the witness responds. Do they answer the question you asked? Do they add extra detail beyond the question? How many words does it take for them to answer the question? Are they confident in their answers? As the answers to these questions become clear, the lawyer will be able to form a list of the preparation areas that must be addressed and a general idea of the effort required.

The lawyer must then determine what role the witness will play in the case. Witnesses that play a key role in the story development require more preparation time and effort than witnesses only tangentially involved. The lawyer should consider whether other witnesses will provide the same or similar information, and whether the trier of fact will expect to hear from the witness. The answer to these types of questions will dictate the level of effort required.

Be careful when making this assessment. Early in a case it is often hard to know what issues will be the most important by the time the case develops fully. To be safe, the lawyer should develop a standard set of preparation materials that can be used to prepare all witnesses. At a minimum, these materials will include references to the important documents identified in the discovery process. Since the important documents will come from a variety of sources, be sure to mark the references in the preparation materials with the document sources and the level of confidentiality that has been assigned to the documents. Witnesses may not be allowed to see certain materials produced by the other side or third parties under the terms of the protective order governing the case. And, remember that all documents shown to a witness might be discoverable by the other side if those documents refresh the recollection of the witness.

The standard preparation materials must cover the entire case—legal theories and relevant facts. Not all of these preparation materials will be used with every witness. Choices will be made based on the witness's areas of involvement. Details of the witness's connection to the events in the case should be included as well as references to the witness in the documents produced by all sources in the case. Reviewing those documents referencing the witness[1] provides the clearest indication of likely areas of knowledge and, accordingly, areas to be covered in the preparation process.

These preparation materials need to be updated continually as additional information is gathered. When multiple depositions are taking place in a relatively short time, the lawyer must have a system to communicate newly discovered information among all team members involved in witness preparation efforts. With every deposition taken, there is either a new piece of information that is important to the case or a new theory from the other side of the case that needs to explored with future witnesses. Make sure that the lawyers take the time to share those items.

Q 10.2 What's the right approach to preparing a witness?

As with most questions asked in this book, there is no single, definitive right way to approach the witness preparation process. Every preparation session will be affected by the answers to questions answered during the witness assessment process. There are, however, two fundamentally different approaches that should be considered. One approach, let's call it the Traditional Approach, seeks to minimize the words spoken by the witness. A second approach, let's call it the Newer Approach, seeks to have the witness behave in a more normal setting. And, of course, the best approach in any given situation may well be a blending of both approaches.

Q 10.2.1 How does the Traditional Approach work?

The primary focus of the Traditional Approach is to limit the amount of information conveyed during the deposition. The hallmark of the advice given to the witness is that the "less said the better." Analogies are often made to sporting events by telling the witness that they are only playing defense during the deposition. The witness should not seek opportunities to advance case themes or stories, and no matter what, should only answer the question asked without volunteering any additional information beyond what the question asked. This mantra is often highlighted with an exchange focused on time. If the question asked is, "Do you know the time?," the correct answer is not to give the time but only to answer yes or no depending on whether the witness has knowledge of the time.

Under the Traditional Approach, the witness may be given four answers to consider as the right response to any closed question they are asked—yes, no, I don't know, or I don't remember. The witness will be reminded that the deposition process is not a conversation and that they should feel no obligation to try to keep the conversation going. When a question has been answered, the witness should stop talking and should not speak until another question is asked. The witness should also avoid guessing about an answer. If the answer is not readily clear to the witness, the right answer is "I don't know" or "I can't remember." This instruction is often highlighted by reminding the witness that they have taken an oath to tell the truth and that guessing about an answer can lead to a violation of the oath leading to potential perjury charges.

These rules can be hard to follow for any witness. And, if followed by all witnesses, the party may find itself with no witness capable of testifying about key areas of the case. A witness that did not know about an area of the case at their deposition will be subjected to a very heavy cross-examination if they have a vivid recollection of events at trial. (For each new detail, the witness will be asked if they remembered that detail at the time of their deposition. The deposition transcript will be displayed to the jury with the various "I don't know" answers highlighted. The more of those answers the witness has, the easier it is for the cross-examining lawyer to demonstrate that the witness has conveniently remembered helpful information only at trial. Such a witness is not likely to be trusted by the jury.) The party may also find it hard to support key elements of a summary judgment motion if its witnesses have not been able to recall the needed information during discovery.

Q 10.2.2 What is different about the Newer Approach?

The Newer Approach recognizes that over 95% of litigation matters settle or are resolved through motion practice. However, the terms of the pretrial resolution are influenced by the results of discovery. To achieve a favorable pretrial resolution, a party must demonstrate the strength of its case to the other side. And, strength of a case is measured, largely, by the strength of the witnesses testifying for a party.

To increase the strength of the witness testimony, the Newer Approach emphasizes having witnesses be more forthcoming. While the witness will still be encouraged not to volunteer information, the focus is on answering questions truthfully, leaving no false impressions. In doing so, the witness will generally advance the key elements of the client's story within their personal knowledge and will try to answer the "spirit" of the question asked. And, the witness will only be guided to not recall an answer if they have no recollection of the events being asked. Instead of answering with "I don't recall," the witness will answer the question with whatever qualifications necessary to make the answer the witness's best recollection of the events underlying the question.

The Newer Approach is easier for witnesses to follow. The witness can rely on normal conversational skills, but they must still be reminded to keep the discussion within the boundaries of what the questioner is asking. Paying attention to the questions asked remains a primary concern.

Q 10.3 What are the ethical rules governing witness preparation?

Regardless of the witness preparation approach selected, the preparing lawyer must abide by the governing rules of ethics. The guiding rule is found in Model Rule of Professional Responsibility 3.3(a)(3): "A lawyer shall not knowingly offer evidence that the lawyer knows to be false."[2] And, in civil cases, the rule provides that "a lawyer may refuse to offer evidence . . . that the lawyer reasonably believes is false." In preparing a witness, the question the lawyer must always answer is whether he or she "knows" the testimony offered by the witness is false. And, the lawyer must avoid suggesting to the witness an answer the lawyer knows to be false. The hard issue for the lawyer is determining when the witness's answer is false. Making that determination requires the lawyer to make assessments of the witness's demeanor and the words chosen. The lawyer must also know the context of prior discussions that preceded the witness's answer to assess the impact, if any, that the prior conversations with the witness have had on the answer given. The witness should be given the benefit of any doubts. Accusing the witness of lying will not advance the trust required for a successful witness preparation session. Nevertheless, remember that the final judgment as to the witness's credibility during the deposition will be made by a judge should the issue ever come to their attention. As a result, care must be taken to assess questions objectively. And, because it is often hard for the lawyer on the case to have a completely objective view, seeking the advice of a trusted third party may be beneficial.

The ethical rules provide no further guidance on witness preparation. The Section of Litigation of the American Bar Association prepared Ethical Guidelines for witness preparation in 2011. Those proposed guidelines have yet to be adopted or approved by the Board of Governors of the American Bar Association and remain in draft form. But the ABA does recommend the guidelines as a "resource designed to facilitate and promote ethical conduct in witness preparation."[3]

The Litigation Section's Draft Guidelines confirm that "a lawyer has a duty to prepare a witness to testify." The preparation may include discussion of how the law applies to the events in the case, but in doing so "the attorney must respect the important ethical distinction between discussing testimony and seeking improperly to influence it."[4] The Guidelines make clear that the lawyer may provide the witness with questions that are likely to be asked, describe the deposition process, and caution against unsuccessfully long answers.[5] The lawyer may also assist the witness by identifying potential responses to questions that are misleading, confusing, or likely to be misconstrued.[6] And, the lawyer may suggest particularly powerful language or other ways for the witness to convey their meaning.[7]

The overriding limitation on the lawyer's conduct remains the truth. The lawyer may not suggest testimony that would be false or misleading.[8] Lawyers may not use their questions during preparation sessions to suggest an answer that the witness does not recall, but the lawyer may have to challenge a witness statement that the lawyer believes to be false based on other information.[9] The duty to challenge a believed false statement goes to the core of the duty to represent the witness. The witness should not be allowed to testify to a fact that other evidence suggests is false.

Q 10.3.1 How do you apply these ethical rules in practice?

As with all matters related to depositions, application of these ethical principles becomes easier with practice. Even the beginner should feel safe covering the following:

- Describe for the witness the deposition room, the players, and how the deposition process works;
- Provide the witness with the areas of inquiry that they should expect, along with types of questions that might be asked;
- Explain to the witness the purpose behind various questions that might be asked and their relationship to issues in the case;
- Explain the dangers to the witness of providing long, narrative answers;
- Demonstrate ways in which various answers may be used by the other side in support of their case, and suggest better ways of expressing the witness's testimony that are still truthful;[10] and

- Assist the witness in conveying the "fair meaning" of their testimony—aid in recalling and describing the truth as opposed to creating a "new" truth.

Q 10.3.2 How do you cover these topics in a way that the witness will be able to carry the preparation into the deposition room?

The skill for the practitioner to learn is how to create a conversation that reinforces key principles in a repetitive fashion without insulting the witness's intelligence or trying their patience. The best advice is to vary the preparation session into several distinctive segments. First, the lawyer must be clear on who the lawyer represents. The witness may not be the client, but the lawyer may represent the witness for the deposition if there are no conflicts. Assuming the witness will have the lawyer represent him for the deposition, the main topic to cover in this discussion is that you will have an attorney-client relationship with the witness, but that you also have such a relationship with the client you represent in the litigation. Why is that important? The witness must know that you will not, and cannot, keep information shared with you confidential from the client you represent. If this conversation raises a problem, the witness may need separate representation.[11]

Second, the lawyer must establish rapport with the witness. Different lawyers will approach this process differently, but the suggestion is not to begin with a serious discussion of the issues of the case and the witness's role. Rather, begin the process with an effort to assess the witness's concerns about the upcoming deposition and with the case.

The witness cannot listen to the information the lawyer seeks to convey until their concerns and fears have been addressed. Some witnesses will come to the preparation session fearful of embarrassment or even potential loss of job. The lawyer's job is to listen to the witness as they discuss their concerns. Resist the temptation to rush through that process. The witness will sense whether the lawyer shows genuine concern for their issues. By showing that concern, the witness will begin to trust the lawyer and be more receptive to the lawyer's suggestions during the preparation process. The lawyer must use his or her skills to make sure to exhaust the witness's areas of concern. Do not just create a list of issues. Ask questions that establish why the issue is a concern to the witness. Knowing why the witness is worried about an issue will help guide the lawyer's preparation session and will provide him or her with valuable insight into the way the witness thinks about issues.

The lawyer does not always have the ability to make all concerns go away. Do not promise the witness results that cannot be guaranteed. If the witness is concerned about his or her job, for example, the lawyer does not control that decision.[12] (Be aware that sometimes a witness can wind up abandoning the deposition game plan generated during witness preparation sessions and instead provide answers—with the goal of defending and protecting him/herself—that can come across as evasive, defensive, and argumentative, and often open a new "can of worms" that expose the witness, and subsequent witnesses, to further attack.)[13]

Nor can the lawyer promise that the opposing lawyer will not cover an area during the deposition. Instead, stay within the framework of reassuring the witness of the deposition rules and how those rules can work to their advantage to stay in control of the deposition process.

Third, the discussion of concerns and anxieties provides a segue to the discussion of the rules for the deposition process. Remember that merely reciting a series of rules for the witness will not suffice. The witness will not be able to absorb the stated rule and apply it to the deposition process without some practice. The amount of practice required will vary by witness. But the fourth and final part of the preparation process is to go back and forth between practice and reminding the witness of the rules.

Q 10.3.3 What deposition rules should be covered with a witness?

Always tell the truth.

Every experienced lawyer will have a different view on what is the right set of guidelines that should be given to a witness. All should agree that the witness must know that they must tell the truth in response to the questions asked. This point must be emphasized at multiple points during the preparation session. Never let the witness think that you are attempting to get them to say anything other than the truth. The witness also must know that they are the only one in the room sworn to tell the truth. Accordingly, they should not assume that the lawyer asking questions is telling them the truth through the questions being asked. To the contrary, the lawyer asking questions hopes that his questions will become truth because they have been accepted by the witness.

To avoid this trap, the witness must listen carefully to every question asked. The witness is not conversing with the lawyer asking questions. The witness should pause long enough to make sure that they have heard the question and had time to formulate an answer. Sometimes the witness will need an example to help make this process understandable. One such example is to suggest the witness diagram the question in his or her mind. The diagram will focus on identifying the subject of the question and then the first three or four words of the sentence because those words normally tell the witness what the lawyer wants to know about that subject. In the process of diagraming the sentence, the witness should look for adjectives, qualifiers, or other miscellaneous words that qualify the subject in the question. As those qualifiers are identified, the witness must decide whether those qualifiers are truthful. If not, the diagram process can stop and the witness should identify the qualifiers that are inaccurate.

The witness should not talk until that internal diagraming process is complete. The time it takes for the witness to review the question allows the defending lawyer time to insert an objection to the question if required. Pausing also prevents the deposing lawyer from developing a rapid pace to the examination that might lead the witness into answering without giving the requisite thought to each question.

It may be a perfect time to remind the witness that each question and answer can stand on their own. The lawyer asking questions does not have to group all questions on a topic together. Instead, the lawyer may use an isolated question and answer. While the other side can always provide a complete picture of the testimony, the better position is to avoid creating the opportunity for an isolated question and answer. Thus, if the answer to a question relies on answers already given, the witness should reference such other answers in responding to the new question.

Keep answers short.

The witness should be advised to answer the question with the shortest possible truthful answer. Some witnesses will believe that they if they could provide a full explanation of the issue being asked about, the deposing lawyer will agree with them and dismiss the case. Remind the witness that the lawyer asking questions is being paid to ask questions and to make the best possible case for their client. As a result, the lawyer asking questions will not likely be dissuaded during the deposition. The far more likely result is that the witness's more expansive answers will raise issues that the questioning lawyer had not thought of prior to the deposition. The end result is more questions, not a concession.

Acceptable answers include: yes, no, I don't know, or I can't remember. Those answers should only be used, however, if they are the shortest possible, truthful answer to the question. If a qualification is required, the witness should also provide that, but the qualification should also be brief.

Ask for clarification.

The witness may ask the questioner to clarify questions before answering. If the witness does not understand the question, asking a question about the question may be the best answer. The witness should know that the questioning lawyer will likely ask additional questions before providing any clarification. For example, if the witness says, "I don't understand the question," the questioner will often ask the witness, "What don't you understand about the question?" Similarly, if the witness questions the meaning of a word in the question, the questioner will often ask the witness to define the meaning of the word and then answer the question using that definition. This may seem like gamesmanship, and it may be. But, the questioner does not want to encourage the witness to avoid the questions asked. Nevertheless, if the witness does not understand what he or she is being asked to testify about, the proper response is to either to ask for a clarification or state he or she does not understand the question.

The witness should not overuse this right to ask questions. A repeated pattern of asking questions about the questions asked will be viewed as an effort to avoid the deposition process. If severe enough, the behavior can result in a request for sanctions and likely a longer deposition process.

Avoid becoming emotional.

Some questioners will seek to provoke emotional responses from the witness. Fear, embarrassment, and anger are among the more effective emotions for a questioner to create in the witness. These emotions make the witness want to strike back at the questioner. Striking back is dangerous, and if the witness is getting agitated, he or she may need a break in the deposition to regain the proper composure.

An emotional witness loses focus on answering the question and may even exaggerate the answer to "win" the argument with the questioning lawyer. The witness cannot win the argument. The questioning lawyer will, however, focus on the exaggeration, the misstatement, and seek to undermine the witness's credibility.

When the witness is an executive in an organization, the questioner will begin the deposition by focusing on the witness's position in the organization and establishing the importance of a person in that position being aware of what transpires in the organization. Then, the questioner will generally focus on a specific detail of a key part of the case and ask the executive to explain that detail. The executive may not remember the details surrounding that fact but, by playing up the executive's role and importance, the executive may be unwilling to admit their lack of knowledge. What happens next can be very dangerous to the executive. The executive may rationalize an answer based on his or her assumptions of what must have happened. The executive may feel confident in doing so based on his or her long experience with the organization and its operations. But, the executive need miss only a detail to find him/herself in trouble. The truthful response that the executive does not recall will serve the witness, and the case, far better.

Advise the witness to avoid letting emotions take control of his or her responses, unless the question attacks the witness's personal integrity. Questions that accuse the witness of lying, cheating, or stealing must be met with a strong, emotional denial. Lack of emotion in response to such a charge will not be perceived as credible. The key, however, is that the witness must then let the emotion subside for the next question which does not contain such a personal integrity attack.

Avoid absolutes unless absolutely true.

Advise the witness to focus carefully on questions that ask for information in absolute terms. Questions like "Have you or your company ever done X?" invariably are difficult for a witness to answer. First, the witness may not possess the knowledge to answer such a question if he or she has not been with the company since its inception; it is even more unlikely that the witness has followed every single employee of the company since its inception. Second, human memory lacks the ability to retain information for such broad ranging questions. Accordingly, the witness should watch out for questions that contain words like always, never, ever, and all.

The witness should answer such questions in a way that restricts the answer to the witness's knowledge. For example, "to the best of my knowledge, the company has not done X." Other times, an equally true answer may be a simple "I don't know." Alternatively, the witness can identify his or her inability to answer a broad question because the witness lacks the information to do so.

Keep control of the pace of the questioning.

Witnesses often believe that the lawyer asking questions controls the deposition. After all, the lawyer is the one asking questions and tells the witness the rules that will be followed during the deposition process. The natural assumption is that the lawyer controls the pace of the questioning. Skilled deposing lawyers will seek to exercise that control by asking questions quickly, sometimes asking another question before the witness finishes answering the first question. Lawyers will also seek to increase the pace of their questions to see if the witness will adopt the faster pace. The faster a witness answers questions, the less time the witness has to think about the question and the answer, and the more likely he or she is to agree with a statement they would otherwise question if they had taken more time to consider it.

The witness, however, possesses complete control over the pace at which he or she answers questions. Train the witness to take each question as a separate event, unconnected to any prior question. Each question must be examined on its own merit and answered. The time to listen to each question and formulate a response should give the witness total control over the deposition pace. And, the witness should be encouraged to inform the questioner if he or she has not finished answering a prior question before trying to answer another question. The process of review and contemplating a response gives the witness total control. But, expect the need to remind the witness of this more than once during a long deposition.

Answer only that which was asked.

Witnesses believe that if they can only explain their side of the case, the other party will be convinced of the truth of their position. This strategy never works. Instead, the helpful witness provides the questioning lawyer with additional areas of inquiry and time to consider the response to the story being told.

This does not mean that the witness should not answer the question being asked. Quite the contrary, rule number one for all witnesses is to answer the question truthfully. But, the witness should not answer more than is asked. Besides making sure the witness understands that the questioning lawyer will not be convinced to drop the case based on the witness's testimony, provide the witness with a motivation to only answer the question that has been asked. One example of motivation is to remind the witness that longer answers will only serve to make the deposition go longer than the questioning lawyer had planned. A good questioning lawyer listens to the answers that are given and looks for additional areas to explore based on those answers. The result is additions to the outline and a longer deposition.

A helpful analogy is to suggest that the witness view the deposition process as entering a long hallway. The exit sign is barely visible at the end of the hallway and represents the end of the deposition. Along the hallway are a number of doors. Each door represents a question on the outline of the questioning lawyer. As a question gets asked, the witness places their hand on the doorknob and decides whether to open the door or not. A door is opened when information not required to answer the question truthfully is provided. An open door leads the deposition out of the hallway and the deposition cannot be completed until the questioner returns to the hallway. The rooms off the hallway vary in size. Some are very small broom closets, but others might be as large as a sports stadium. The witness is well advised to resist the urge to twist the doorknob and to leave the door closed.

Like Entering A Hallway

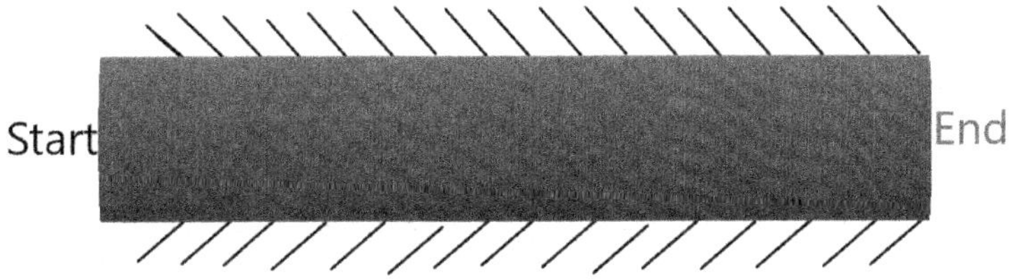

Like all rules, there are some exceptions for certain witnesses. In each case, there are a few key witnesses with the most relevant knowledge of the facts of the case from the defending lawyer's perspective. These witnesses need to have special training to make sure that they adequately disclose the facts as they know them to be. Some might say to save that information until trial. Years ago, this author would have agreed. But, the reality today is that the overwhelming majority of cases settle or are disposed of by the court well before trial. As a result, the defending lawyer will want to ensure that the questioning lawyer has an adequate basis to assess the appropriate value of the case. Choose the witness to carry this burden carefully and, if there is not a good one for the job, apply the normal rule.

What to do with objections.

Lawyer objections confuse witnesses. Avoid that confusion by making sure that the witness knows about the objection process. Tell the witness not to be distracted when objections are made or by any commentary between the lawyers that may take place during the deposition. This will be hard for the witness, but the witness should remain focused on the question. The only exception to this rule is when the lawyer instructs the witness not to answer the question. The witness should be told to follow their lawyer's advice and not answer if instructed not to do so.[14] The defending lawyer should have a brief conversation with the witness during preparation about privilege issues because the witness may not realize conversations with their lawyers are privileged in most circumstances. The witness must always alert the defending lawyer if an answer might involve a revelation of a conversation with another lawyer because the defending lawyer might not have been previously aware of such conversation. If the deposition is of a lawyer, then this discussion will be much more detailed and will require greater discussion of the law of privilege.

Objections also give the witness time to consider the question more carefully and to determine whether the lawyer's objection highlights a particular problem with the question. And, the witness needs to remember to allow the defending lawyer time to raise an objection before answering the question.

Q 10.3.4 What else should you do in the preparation process?

Witnesses need to practice the deposition process. The lawyer must take them through sample questions the deposing lawyer will likely cover and listen to how the witness responds. After several minutes of this process, the lawyer should stop the sample questions and review the rules that the witness failed to follow. As the rules are discussed, the lawyer should show witness a proper way to handle the question and explain why the answer given could create problems during the deposition.

Practice time varies with every witness. Some will need a lot more time than others. The key is to make sure the witness has incorporated the basic preparation information. The danger is that the lawyer creates a witness that is so anxious that he or she struggles to answer any question and loses credibility. Again, the lawyer's judgment must be exercised to determine when the witness is ready to testify.

Defending the Deposition

Q 10.4 What should the lawyer defending the deposition worry about?

The defending lawyer worries about everything, but has little power to change the outcome once the deposition begins. The hard work should be done during the pre-deposition preparation session. On the morning of the deposition, the defending lawyer will spend his or her time making sure the witness is comfortable by addressing any last minute questions the witness may have.

If the deposition is not taking place at the defending lawyer's office, schedule to meet the witness at another location and go to the deposition together. Never take the chance that the witness will arrive at the deposition room before the defending lawyer. The risk that the witness will engage in a conversation with the taking lawyer or somebody on the other side is too high. The defending lawyer does not want the witness to become too friendly with the deposing lawyer or with the representative of the other side.[15]

Once the witness and the defending lawyer arrive at the deposition site, the defending lawyer will want to make sure that the deposition room arrangements are acceptable. The defending lawyer will focus on the comfort of the chair, the room lighting, the temperature, and the location of the court reporter and, if there is one, of the videographer. Make sure that none of these conditions will distract the witness from the task at hand. If changes are required, insist those changes take place before the deposition begins.

Q 10.4.1 What should the defending lawyer focus on once the deposition begins?

The primary role is to support the witness. This support includes, but is not limited to, making sure the witness remembers how to respond to questions. The defending lawyer will also want to make sure that the small things are handled for the witness. Make sure the witness has a drink, and keep the area around the witness free of clutter. As documents are discussed, create a numerically ordered pile for the court reporter. The defending lawyer should also assist the witness in find ing an earlier exhibit if the questioner refers to a prior exhibit. In short, make sure the witness has nothing to worry about other than answering the questions asked. This task alone will exhaust the witness. The witness draws upon the defending lawyer's presence as moral support during the entire process and needs some positive reassurance that he or she is answering questions appropriately.[16]

Q 10.4.2 What rules govern the start of a deposition from the defending lawyer's perspective?

The defending lawyer needs to make sure that there is a clear agreement on the rules that will govern the taking of the deposition. Rule 30 of the Federal Rules of Civil Procedure imposes one additional requirement on the defending lawyer. Under Rule 30(e), the witness's right to review and sign a deposition transcript is not automatic. The rule requires that a request be made prior to the end of the deposition to preserve that right.[17]

The defending lawyer must also avoid uncertainty over any of the rules that will govern the deposition. Lawyers that have practiced for a long time in a given jurisdiction tend to talk about doing depositions under the "usual stipulations" or some variant of that phrase. When asked, most of these lawyers will have no idea exactly what the "usual stipulations" are. As the defending lawyer, avoid the uncertainty and make sure to use a set of rules, like the federal or state rules where the case is located, that are easy to identify. By knowing the rules that govern the deposition, the defending lawyer will know the rules governing objections.

Q 10.4.3 What are the rules governing objections to questions at depositions?

FRCP 30(c)(2) provides:

> Objections. An objection at the time of the examination—whether to evidence, to a party's conduct, to the officer's qualifications, to the manner of taking the deposition, or to any other aspect of the deposition—must be noted on the record, but the examination still proceeds; the testimony is taken subject to any objection. An objection must be stated concisely in a nonargumentative and nonsuggestive manner. A person may instruct a deponent not to answer only when necessary to preserve a privilege, to enforce a limitation ordered by the court, or to present a motion under Rule 30(d)(3).

Generally, the rules require that objections to questions or activities that could be corrected during the deposition must be made during the deposition. The rule prevents one party from "laying behind the log" and raising an issue only after the error can no longer be corrected. Applied to depositions, objections to the form of a question are the most common example of objections waived unless raised when the objectionable question is asked. Rule 30(c) also requires contemporaneous objections to the conduct of any party at the deposition, the qualifications of the court reporter or videographer, any problems with the room, or any other issue that might affect the witness's testimony. Unless the issue is so serious that the defending lawyer moves for a protective order to prevent the deposition from proceeding, the deposition proceeds and the court will resolve the objection after the deposition is concluded.

Turning to the actual deposition questioning, the defending lawyer must avoid "speaking" objections—objections that serve more to provide answers to the witness than they do to fairly object to the question asked. Historically, questions would be asked and the defending lawyer would engage in a lengthy objection that would contain instructions to the witness on how to answer the question.[18] The rules were amended to clarify that such conduct was no longer permissible. Jurisdictions vary in how this rule is implemented. Some jurisdictions only permit the use of the phrase "objection to form" with no further explanation unless requested by the lawyer taking the deposition. Other jurisdictions require that the objection contain at least enough for the questioner to understand the nature of the objection. *See* Appendix A. The only safe course is to make sure that the defending lawyer understands the rules that apply to the deposition.

Q 10.4.4 How does the defending lawyer protect privileges during the deposition?

The defending lawyer must protect all possible privileges held by his or her client and the witness. The lawyer must be sensitive to these privilege issues because once the witness discloses a privilege matter the privilege is waived. To avoid these situations, part of the witness preparation is to remind the witness to be sensitive to the possibility of revealing a privileged communication. During the deposition, the witness should say "I need to talk to my lawyer to make sure I do not reveal anything that might be privileged" or something similar. The defending lawyer then calls a break in the deposition and discusses the privilege issue with the witness outside the presence of all other parties. Once a decision is made on whether a privilege is invoked, the lawyer and the witness return to the room and the defending lawyer should state on the record whether a claim of privilege is being asserted. If a claim is being asserted, the defending lawyer should then state that the lawyer is instructing the witness not to answer the question and assert the privilege being asserted.

Without attempting to exhaust areas of privilege, the defending lawyer should focus on attorney-client privilege and work product protection. Work product most often comes up in a deposition when the witness is asked whether he or she reviewed documents in the course of preparing for the deposition. If the answer is yes and those documents were selected by counsel, a work product doctrine claim may be asserted. The theory of the objection is that the documents counsel selected for the witness to review reflect the lawyer's mental impressions. Of course, the work product doctrine may be overcome in some cases. As it relates to the review of documents in preparation for a deposition, Federal Rule of Evidence 612 provides that documents that refreshed the witness's memory may be a proper subject of discovery.

Do not be surprised if the taking lawyer asks the witness if they will follow the instruction. Similarly, do not be surprised if the taking lawyer asks questions designed to determine whether the claim of privilege can be overcome. For example, questions about who the witness met with, for how long, where they met, and were other people in attendance when a privileged communication occurred, are all fair game. The tricky part for the defending lawyer is making sure that the witness sticks to those details in their answers and does not divulge the substance of the privileged communication.

Q 10.4.5 May the defending lawyer confer with the witness once the deposition has begun?

The answer depends on the jurisdiction. In several jurisdictions, the deposition is treated just like testimony at trial, and the defending lawyer may not talk to the witness about the substance of their testimony once the deposition starts. Delaware is a prime example of this practice. Under Delaware Chancery Court Rule 30(d)(1):

> From the commencement until the conclusion of a deposition, including any recesses or continuances thereof of less than five calendar days, the attorney(s) for the deponent shall not: (A) consult or confer with the deponent regarding the substance of the testimony already given or anticipated to be given, except for the

> purpose of conferring on whether to assert a privilege against testifying or on how to comply with a court order, or (B) suggest to the deponent the manner in which any questions should be answered. A person may instruct a deponent not to answer only when necessary to preserve a privilege, to enforce a limitation on evidence directed by the Court, or to present a motion under paragraph (d)(3).

The ban on consulting with the witness applies to testimony that has been given as well as any anticipated testimony. But the rule is not just limited to areas of testimony; the defending lawyer is also prohibited from suggesting the manner in which questions should be answered. In short, with the exception of matters relating to privilege or complying with orders of the court, the defending lawyer may not talk to the witness about the deposition until it is concluded.

Other jurisdictions do not impose such a strict limitation and allow the defending lawyer, during breaks in the deposition, to discuss with the witness his or her testimony, including areas that may need to be clarified, as well as the manner in which the witness is answering questions.

Again, a defending lawyer should make sure to know the rules that apply to the deposition. *See* Appendix A.

Q 10.5 What should the defending lawyer avoid during the deposition?

The defending lawyer must make sure not to obstruct the fair asking of questions of the witness. Fairness is often hard to articulate, but there is no question that defending lawyers have been increasingly subjected to sanctions for their deposition conduct in recent years. The reasons for this trend are hard to identify, but one source has suggested that courts realize the very important role that depositions play in civil litigation.[19] Other courts are simply fed up with what they view as an obstructionist attitude that predominates in modern litigation.[20]

There are not absolute standards for determining whether the defending lawyer's conduct should be sanctioned. One thing that is clear, however, is that courts do not want repeated objections during the deposition. The total number of objections may be enough for the court to order sanctions. And, this is more likely to occur if the objections have an effect on the witness. When the witness adopts the language used by the lawyer in an objection as part of his or her response to a question, the court is likely to assume that objection was made for an improper purpose.

The best advice to the defending lawyer is to pick and choose the questions to which objections are raised. Do not object to all questions that might have some objectionable problem. And, be sure to tell the witness that they are to answer the question asked of them unless they are specifically instructed not to answer.

Notes to Chapter 10

1. Guidelines for reviewing documents are not part of this book, but documents that mention a witness should be categorized in area of importance by the role that the witness played in the document's creation and circulation. Documents that were authored by the witness should have first priority since the witness will be expected to have a greater knowledge of information contained in documents they wrote. Documents in which the witness is a direct recipient should have the second highest priority since the witness was clearly informed of the information in the document. As the witness moves further down the list of recipients, the priority of the document will also drop, except for the key documents in the case. If a witness is mentioned in a key document, that document must be part of the preparation materials for that witness.

2. The rule goes on to impose a requirement on lawyers to take "reasonable remedial measures" to correct a client that the lawyer knows to be false.

3. Draft Section of Litigation, American Bar Association, "Ethical Guidelines for Witness Preparation 2011–2012," at 2, https://www.americanbar.org/content/dam/aba/administrative/litigation/links/aba-ethical-witness-prepartion-guidelines.authcheckdam.pdf.

4. *Id.* at 9 (section 1.1), quoting Geders v. United States, 425 U.S. 80, 90 n.3 (1978).

5. *Id.* at 9 (section 1.2).

6. *Id.*

7. *Id.*

8. *Id.* at 9–10 and n.14. Note 14 contains a lengthy reference to a memorandum prepared by a plaintiffs' firm in the asbestos litigation entitled "Preparing for Your Deposition." *See, e.g.*, Abner v. Elliot, 706 N.E.2d 765, 767 (Ohio 1999) and S. Rep. No. 108-118 (July 21, 1993). The central problem with this memorandum, from an ethics standpoint, was that it provided advice to all potential witnesses on how to answer questions without any particular focus on the individual witness's knowledge.

9. *Id.* at 11.

10. Obviously, this is an area where the ethical rules discussed in this chapter will come into play. The purpose should be to help the witness clarify their answers in such a way as to improve the clarity of the answers given without affecting the truthfulness of those answers. One way to accomplish this in an ethical way is to ask the witness to explain their answer in more detail. Listen carefully to the explanation and see if there are words used in that explanation that might make the original answer clear.

11. Separate representation raises the side issue of who will pay for that separate counsel. Sometimes it will be in the lawyer's client's interests to do so. But other times, the lawyer's client may elect to distance themselves from the witness and, absent some obligation to do so, will not pay for the separate counsel. The risk that arises is that the witness may choose not to pay for a separate lawyer and not be prepared for the deposition.

12. On rare occasions, an issue may be so sensitive that the lawyer will decide to seek a protective order precluding the issue from being addressed during discovery. Such a motion should only be made if there is a high probability that it will be successful. Otherwise, the other side will be on full notice of the issue and of its sensitivity to the witness.

13. *See* Bill Kanasky, Jr., Melissa Loberg & Alyssa Parker, *The Effective Deponent—Preventing Amygdala Hijack*, COURTROOM SCIENCES INC., http://www.courtroomsciences.com/News/Articles/07588d73-3740-48f0-b803-4204c74e3745. The authors explain that a witness might deviate from the deposition plan when he or she experiences an "amygdala hijack"—a term coined by Daniel Goleman in his 1996 book, *Emotional Intelligence: Why It Can Matter More Than IQ*—during deposition, the amygdala (the area of the brain in which the fight or flight reaction is housed) overtakes the prefrontal cortex (the area of the brain responsible for logic and judgment) rendering the witness unable to rely on strategic responses learned in witness preparation sessions. When this occurs, the hypothalamus releases stress hormones into the bloodstream that can take hours to clear, and working memory is essentially halted.

14. The questioning lawyer should always ask witnesses if they will follow the instructions of their lawyer to avoid any later claim that they have waived their right to challenge the instruction not to answer.

15. The assumption is that the deposing lawyer will not try to talk to the witness about the substance of the case prior to the defending lawyer arriving but rather that the deposing lawyer will do his or her best to establish some basic connection with the witness by finding something they share in common.

16. Whatever conversations the defending lawyer has with the witness should comply with the rules governing the deposition. Some jurisdictions prohibit conversation about the substance of the testimony or the manner in which questions should be answered once the deposition begins.

17. FRCP 30(e) Review by the Witness; Changes.

> (1) *Review; Statement of Changes.* On request by the deponent or a party before the deposition is completed, the deponent must be allowed 30 days after being notified by the officer that the transcript or recording is available in which:
>
> (A) to review the transcript or recording; and
>
> (B) if there are changes in form or substance, to sign a statement listing the changes and the reasons for making them.

(2) *Changes Indicated in the Officer's Certificate.* The officer must note in the certificate prescribed by Rule 30(f)(1) whether a review was requested and, if so, must attach any changes the deponent makes during the 30-day period.

18. The provision requiring objections be short and in a nonargumentative manner was added originally to paragraph d addressing sanctions in the 1993 amendments. As explained in the comments at the time, "[d]epositions frequently have been unduly prolonged, if not unfairly frustrated, by lengthy objections and colloquy, often suggesting how the deponent should respond. While objections may, under the revised rule, be made during a deposition, they ordinarily should be limited to those that under Rule 32(d)(3) might be waived if not made at that time, *i.e.*, objections on grounds that might be immediately obviated, removed, or cured, such as to the form of a question or the responsiveness of an answer."

19. Markowitz & Franco, *Sanctions for Deposition Misconduct*, Or. State Bar's Litig. J. (Spring 2014), https://www.markowitzherbold.com/press-room/Articles/Sanctions-for-Deposition-Misconduct. The authors state:

> Our research revealed a several hundred percent increase in the number of Rule 30(d)(2) sanctions opinions in the last ten years, over the number of opinions in the initial ten years following the Rule's amendment in 1993. Indeed, we identified more opinions concerning Rule 30(d)(2) sanctions in the last two years than in the ten years after 1993. This increase in the use of sanctions for deposition misconduct, as well as the reasoning and tenor of recent judicial opinions, suggests that courts are granting motions for sanctions with increasing frequency.
>
> Judicial willingness to impose sanctions for deposition misconduct may be based in part upon an understanding of how critically important the deposition has become in modern litigation. More than 98% of all civil cases filed in the federal courts result in disposition by way of settlement or pretrial adjudication. Very often, these results turn on evidence obtained during depositions. Thus, depositions play an extremely important role in the American system of justice.

20. *See, e.g.*, Sec. Nat'l Bank of Sioux City, Iowa v. Abbott Labs., 299 F.R.D. 595 (N.D. Iowa 2014), *rev'd*, 800 F.3d 936 (8th Cir. 2015). "Discovery—a process intended to facilitate the free flow of information between parties—is now too often mired in obstructionism. Today's 'litigators' are quick to dispute discovery requests, slow to produce information, and all-too-eager to object at every stage of the process. They often object using boilerplate language containing every objection imaginable, despite the fact that courts have resoundingly disapproved of such boilerplate objections. Some litigators do this to grandstand for their client, to intentionally obstruct the flow of clearly discoverable information, to try and win a war of attrition, or to intimidate and harass the opposing party. Others do it simply because it's how they were taught."

Appendix A

*State Rules on Depositions**

* Current as of August 2018.

State/Territory	Presumptive Number of Depositions	Presumptive Time Limit	Location/Range of Deposition	Rule 30(b)(6) Equivalent	Rules for Defending
Alabama	N/A	N/A	ALA. R. CIV. P. 45(c)(3)(A) May be served anywhere in state. Subpoena may be quashed if it asks resident to travel more than 100 miles from place of residence/employment/regular transaction of business, or if non-resident (non-officer) is 100 miles from place of service or place of employment/business	ALA. R. CIV. P. 30(b)(6)	ALA. R. CIV. P. 30(c) Does not contain limitation of FRCP 30(c) limiting objections to non-argumentative and non-suggestive language
Alaska	ALASKA R. CIV. P. 30(a)(2)(A) Must have court approval before taking more than 3, not including parties, experts, treating physicians, or document custodians	ALASKA R. CIV. P. 30(d)(2) 6 hours for parties, experts, and treating physicians 3 hours for all others	ALASKA R. CIV. P. 45(d)(2) Anywhere within judicial district for resident of district Non-resident of a district or of state anywhere within district of service	ALASKA R. CIV. P. 30(b)(6)	ALASKA R. CIV. P. 30(c) Does not contain limitation of FRCP 30(c) limiting objections to non-argumentative and non-suggestive language

State/Territory	Presumptive Number of Depositions	Presumptive Time Limit	Location/Range of Deposition	Rule 30(b)(6) Equivalent	Rules for Defending
Arizona	N/A	ARIZ. R. CIV. P. 30(d) 4 hours	ARIZ. R. CIV. P. 45(b)(3) Party or a party's officer may be served in county of residence/place of transaction of business; county or service or within 40 miles thereof	ARIZ. R. CIV. P. 30(b)(6)	ARIZ. R. CIV. P. 30(c) Does not contain limitation of FRCP 30(c) limiting objections to non-argumentative and non-suggestive language
Arkansas	N/A	N/A	ARK. R. CIV. P. 45(c) Served anywhere within state Within 100 miles of residence/place of employment/transacts business	ARK. R. CIV. P. 30(b)(6)	ARK. R. CIV. P. 30(d)(1) Objection must be stated concisely and in non-argumentative and non-suggestive manner

State/Territory	Presumptive Number of Depositions	Presumptive Time Limit	Location/Range of Deposition	Rule 30(b)(6) Equivalent	Rules for Defending
California	CAL. CIV. PROC. §§ 94–95 No limit if greater than $25K If less than $25K, then one deposition	CAL. CIV. PROC. § 2025.290 7 hours, unless stipulated otherwise Limit does not apply to experts, cases designated as complex, employee litigation against employer, or of an entity	CAL. CIV. PROC. § 2025.250 Within 75 miles of deponent's residence, or within county where action pending and within 150 miles of deponent's residence	CAL. CIV. PROC. § 2025.230	CAL. CIV. PROC. § 2025.460(b) Objection must be raised to any matter that could be cured at time
Colorado	COLO. R. CIV. P. 26(b)(2)(A) Without court order, may depose each adverse party plus 2 others, excluding experts	COLO. R. CIV. P. 30(d)(2)(A); 26(b)(4)(A) 6 hours	COLO. R. CIV. P. 45 Service anywhere in state A non-party/corporate officer in county of residence/employed/ transacts business in person	COLO. R. CIV. P. 30(b)(6)	COLO. R. CIV. P. 30(d)(1) Objection must be stated concisely and in a non-argumentative manner

State/Territory	Presumptive Number of Depositions	Presumptive Time Limit	Location/Range of Deposition	Rule 30(b)(6) Equivalent	Rules for Defending
Connecticut	N/A	N/A	CONN. SUP. CT. R. 12-29 Resident/party in the county of residence (or within 30 miles) or county where action pending Non-resident or non-party defendant in county of personal service or county of personal residence (or within 30 miles)	CONN. SUP. CT. R. 13-27(b)	CONN. SUP. CT. R. 13-30(b) Objection must be stated succinctly and framed so as not to suggest an answer, and if requested, contain a clear statement of defect in form or any other basis for objection
Delaware	N/A	N/A	DEL. SUP. CT. R. 45 Within state, though party issuing subpoena must avoid imposing "undue burden" on person served	DEL. SUP. CT. R. 30(b)(6)	DEL. SUP. CT. R. 30(c) State rule does not contain limitation of FRCP 30(c) limiting objections to non-argumentative and non-suggestive language, but courts have not allowed suggestive answers and the practice is to restrict comments to objection form

State/Territory	Presumptive Number of Depositions	Presumptive Time Limit	Location/Range of Deposition	Rule 30(b)(6) Equivalent	Rules for Defending
Delaware *(cont'd)*					DEL. SUP. CT. R. 30(d) Prohibits defending lawyer from conferring with witness once deposition commences regarding substance of testimony or suggestions as to manner in which question should be answered (excluding privileged matters). See also Local Federal Ct. Rule 30.6

State/Territory	Presumptive Number of Depositions	Presumptive Time Limit	Location/Range of Deposition	Rule 30(b)(6) Equivalent	Rules for Defending
Florida	N/A	N/A	FLA. R. CIV. P. 410(e) County where person resides/employed/ transacts business	FLA. R. CIV. P. 1.310(b)(6)	FLA. R. CIV. P. 1.310(c) Any objection during a deposition must be stated concisely and in a non-argumentative and non-suggestive manner
Georgia	N/A	N/A	GA. CODE ANN. § 9-11-45(b) County where resides/ employed/transacts business (or within 30 miles)/county where served	GA. CODE ANN. § 9-11-30(b)(6)	GA. CODE ANN. § 9-11-30(c)(2) Does not contain limitation of FRCP 30(c) limiting objections to non-argumentative and non-suggestive language

State/Territory	Presumptive Number of Depositions	Presumptive Time Limit	Location/Range of Deposition	Rule 30(b)(6) Equivalent	Rules for Defending
Hawaii	HAW. R. CIV. P. 30(a)(2) 10 depositions	HAW. R. CIV. P. 30(d)(2) 7 hours	HAW. R. CIV. P. 45 Anywhere in state, but resident may only be compelled within county of residence/employment/transacts business Non-resident only in county where served	HAW. R. CIV. P. 30(b)(6)	HAW. R. CIV. P. 30(d)(1) Objection during a deposition must be stated concisely and in a non-argumentative and non-suggestive manner
Idaho	N/A	N/A	IDAHO R. CIV. P. 45(f) Resident only in county resides/employed/transacts business Non-resident in any county where served	IDAHO R. CIV. P. 30(b)(6)	IDAHO R. CIV. P. 30(c)(2) Does not contain limitation of FRCP 30(c) limiting objections to non-argumentative and non-suggestive language

State/Territory	Presumptive Number of Depositions	Presumptive Time Limit	Location/Range of Deposition	Rule 30(b)(6) Equivalent	Rules for Defending
Illinois	N/A	ILL. SUP. CT. R. 206(d) 3 hours	ILL. SUP. CT. R. 203 County in which deponent resides/ employed/or transacts business Party may also be deposed in county where action pending	ILL. SUP. CT. R. 206(a)(1)	ILL. SUP. CT. R. 206(c)(3) Objections shall be concise, stating the exact legal nature of the objection
Indiana	N/A	N/A	IND. R. TRIAL P. 45(D)(2) Individual resident in county where reside/ employed/transacts business in person Non-resident only in county where served or within 40 miles thereof Non-resident plaintiff in the county where action commenced	IND. R. TRIAL P. 30(b)(6)	IND. R. TRIAL P. 30(c) When there is an objection to a question, the objection and reason therefor shall be noted

State/Territory	Presumptive Number of Depositions	Presumptive Time Limit	Location/Range of Deposition	Rule 30(b)(6) Equivalent	Rules for Defending
Iowa	N/A	N/A	IOWA R. CIV. P. 1.701(5) Depositions may be taken in state or within 100 miles from nearest Iowa point absent court order IOWA R. CIV. P. 1.715(2) Resident with 50 miles of residence/place of employment/transacts business in person	IOWA R. CIV. P. 1.707(5)	IOWA R. CIV. P. 1.708(b) An objection must be stated concisely in a non-argumentative and non-suggestive manner
Kansas	N/A	N/A	KAN. STAT. ANN. § 60-245 May be served anywhere in state but may be quashed if: (1) asks non-party resident to travel more than 100 miles from residence/ employed/transacts business in person	KAN. STAT. ANN. § 60-230(b)(6)	KAN. STAT. ANN. § 60-230(2) An objection must be stated concisely in a non-argumentative and non-suggestive manner

State/Territory	Presumptive Number of Depositions	Presumptive Time Limit	Location/Range of Deposition	Rule 30(b)(6) Equivalent	Rules for Defending
Kansas *(cont'd)*			(2) asks non-resident non-party to travel more than 100 miles from place of service/employed/ transacts business in person Except that person may be commanded to travel to the place of trial		
Kentucky	N/A	N/A	KY. R. CIV. P. 45.04 Resident only in county where resides/employed/ transacts business in person	KY. R. CIV. P. 30.02(6)	KY. R. CIV. P. 30.03 Objection to evidence during a deposition shall be stated concisely and in a non-argumentative and non-suggestive manner

State/Territory	Presumptive Number of Depositions	Presumptive Time Limit	Location/Range of Deposition	Rule 30(b)(6) Equivalent	Rules for Defending
Louisiana	N/A	N/A	LA. CODE CIV. PROC. ANN. art. 1436 Resident only where resides/employed/ transacts business in person Non-resident only in parish where served	LA. CODE CIV. PROC. ANN. art. 1442	LA. CODE CIV. PROC. ANN. art. 1443(b) Objection during a deposition shall be stated concisely and in a non-argumentative and non-suggestive manner Counsel shall cooperate with and be courteous to each other and to the witness and otherwise conduct themselves as required in open court and shall be subject to the power of the court to punish for contempt

State/Territory	Presumptive Number of Depositions	Presumptive Time Limit	Location/Range of Deposition	Rule 30(b)(6) Equivalent	Rules for Defending
Maine	ME. R. CIV. P. 30(a) 5 per party	ME. R. CIV. P. 30(d)(2) 8 hours	ME. R. CIV. P. 45 Served anywhere in state Non-party resident only in county where resides/employed/transacts business in person or 100 miles from any of those Non-party non-resident only where served or 100 miles from there	ME. R. CIV. P. 30(b)(6)	ME. R. CIV. P. 30(d)(1) Objection during a deposition shall be stated concisely and in a non-argumentative and non-suggestive manner
Maryland	N/A	MD. CODE ANN., Deposition—Right to Take § 2-411(b) One 7-hour day	MD. CODE ANN., Deposition—Place § 2-413(a)(1) Non-party resident only in county where resides/employed/engaged in business Non-party non-resident only where served or within 40 miles Party can also be in county where case is pending	MD. CODE ANN., Deposition—Notice § 2-412(d)	MD. CODE ANN., Deposition—Notice § 2-415(h) Grounds of an objection need not be stated unless requested by a party. If the ground of an objection is stated, it shall be stated specifically, concisely, and in a non-argumentative

State/Territory	Presumptive Number of Depositions	Presumptive Time Limit	Location/Range of Deposition	Rule 30(b)(6) Equivalent	Rules for Defending
Maryland (*cont'd*)					and non-suggestive manner. If a party desires to make an objection for the record during the taking of a deposition that reasonably could have the effect of coaching or suggesting to the deponent how to answer, then the deponent, at the request of any party, shall be excused from the deposition during the making of the objection

State/Territory	Presumptive Number of Depositions	Presumptive Time Limit	Location/Range of Deposition	Rule 30(b)(6) Equivalent	Rules for Defending
Massachusetts	N/A	N/A	MASS. R. CIV. P. 45 Resident within 50 miles of residence/employment/ place of business (whichever is closer to location in the subpoena) Non-resident within 50 miles of place served	MASS. R. CIV. P. 30(b)(6)	MASS. R. CIV. P. 30(c)(2) Objection to testimony during a deposition shall be stated concisely and in a non-argumentative and non-suggestive manner
Michigan	N/A	N/A	MICH. R. CIV. P. 2.305(C) County where resides/ employed/transacts business in person	MICH. R. CIV. P. 2.306(B)(5)	MICH. R. CIV. P. 2.306(C)(4)(b) Objection during a deposition must be stated concisely in a civil and non-suggestive manner MICH. R. CIV. P. 2.306(C)(5) Deponent, except for privilege, may not communicate with anyone while question pending

State/Territory	Presumptive Number of Depositions	Presumptive Time Limit	Location/Range of Deposition	Rule 30(b)(6) Equivalent	Rules for Defending
Minnesota	N/A	MINN. R. CIV. P. 30.04(b) One 7-hour day	MINN. R. CIV. P. 45.02(b) and 45.03(c) Subpoena may be served state-wide Subpoena may be quashed if requires non-party to travel outside county reside/employed/ regularly transacts business	MINN. R. CIV. P. 30.02(f)	MINN. R. CIV. P. 30.03 Does not contain limitation of FRCP 30(c) limiting objections to non-argumentative and non-suggestive language
Mississippi	N/A	N/A	MISS. R. CIV. P. 45(b) Resident only in county where resides/employed/ transacts business in person Non-resident only in county where served	MISS. R. CIV. P. 30(b)(6)	MISS. R. CIV. P. 30(c) Does not contain limitation of FRCP 30(c) limiting objections to non-argumentative and non-suggestive language

State/Territory	Presumptive Number of Depositions	Presumptive Time Limit	Location/Range of Deposition	Rule 30(b)(6) Equivalent	Rules for Defending
Missouri	N/A	N/A	MO. R. CIV. P. 57.09 No limitation on location, but for non-party must avoid undue burden or expense	MO. R. CIV. P. 57.03(4)	MO. R. CIV. P. 57.03(d) Does not contain limitation of FRCP 30(c) limiting objections to non-argumentative and non-suggestive language
Montana	MONT. R. CIV. P. 30(a)(2)(A)(i) 10 depositions	MONT. R. CIV. P. 30(d)(1) One 7-hour day	MONT. R. CIV. P. 45(c)(2)(B) Resident within 100 miles of where resides/employed/transacts business in person For an entity, within 100 miles of principal location Non-resident within 100 miles of place of service	MONT. R. CIV. P. 30(b)(6)	MONT. R. CIV. P. 30(c)(2) Objection must be stated concisely in a non-argumentative and non-suggestive manner

State/Territory	Presumptive Number of Depositions	Presumptive Time Limit	Location/Range of Deposition	Rule 30(b)(6) Equivalent	Rules for Defending
Nebraska	N/A	N/A	NEB. REV. STAT. § 25-1227 Witnesses not attend outside county of residence or county where the subpoena served	NEB. DISC. R. § 6-330(b)(6)	NEB. DISC. R. § 6-330(c)(2) Objection must be stated concisely in a non-argumentative and non-suggestive manner
Nevada	N/A	NEV. R. CIV. P. 30(d)(1) One 7-hour day	NEV. R. CIV. P. 45 May quash for undue burden Non-party may quash if more than 100 miles from residence/employment/ regular transacts business	NEV. R. CIV. P. 30(b)(6)	NEV. R. CIV. P. 30(d)(1) Objection must be stated concisely and in a non-argumentative and non-suggestive manner
New Hampshire	N.H. SUP. CT. R. 26(a) No more than 20 total hours	N/A	No limitations	N.H. SUP. CT. R. 26(m)	N.H. SUP. CT. R. 26(k) Imposes fees and costs of motion on losing party to the motion if conduct was frivolous or unreasonable

State/Territory	Presumptive Number of Depositions	Presumptive Time Limit	Location/Range of Deposition	Rule 30(b)(6) Equivalent	Rules for Defending
New Jersey	N/A	N/A	N.J. Ct. R. 4-14-7(b) Resident in county where resides/employed/transacts business in person or 20 miles from residence or employment Non-resident in county where served or 40 miles from place of service	N.J. Ct. R. 4-14-2(c)	N.J. Ct. R. 4-14-3(c) No objection except as to form or privilege. Must include a statement as to why question is objectionable. No objection shall suggest an answer to witness N.J. Ct. R. 4-14-3(f) No communication with witness once witness sworn except for claim of privilege, confidentiality, or prior court order
New Mexico	N/A	N.M. R. Ann. § 1-030(D)(2) One 7-hour day	N.M. R. Ann. § 1-045(B)(3) Within 100 miles of where reside/employed/transacts business	N.M. R. Ann. § 1-030(B)(6)	N.M. R. Ann. § 1-030(D)(1) Objection stated concisely and in non-argumentative and non-suggestive manner

State/Territory	Presumptive Number of Depositions	Presumptive Time Limit	Location/Range of Deposition	Rule 30(b)(6) Equivalent	Rules for Defending
New Mexico (*cont'd*)					Objection form or objection foundation without explanation unless requested No argumentative interruptions permitted and no interruption while question pending except for claim of privilege
New York	N/A	N/A	N.Y. C.P.L.R. 31-3110 Party county where resides/has office/action pending Resident county where resides/employed/office for regular business Non-resident in county where served/employed/office for regular business	N.Y. C.P.L.R. 31-3106(d)	N.Y. C.P.L.R. 31-3115 Objection waived if could have been cured at time by objection Does not contain limitation of FRCP 30(c) limiting objections to non-argumentative and non-suggestive language

State/Territory	Presumptive Number of Depositions	Presumptive Time Limit	Location/Range of Deposition	Rule 30(b)(6) Equivalent	Rules for Defending
North Carolina	N/A	N/A	N.C. GEN. STAT. ANN. § 1A-1-30(b)(1) Resident in county where resides/employed/ transacts business in person Non-resident in county where resides/50 miles of place of service	N.C. GEN. STAT. ANN. § 1A-1-30(b)(6)	N.C. GEN. STAT. ANN. § 1A-1-30(c) Does not contain limitation of FRCP 30(c) limiting objections to non-argumentative and non-suggestive language
North Dakota	N/A	N/A	N.D. R. CIV. P. 45(c)(3) Resident in county where resides/employed/ transacts business Non-resident any county in state	N.D. R. CIV. P. 30(b)(6)	N.D. R. CIV. P. 30(c)(2) Objection must be stated concisely in non-argumentative and non-suggestive manner
Ohio	N/A	N/A	OHIO R. CIV. P. 45(A)(1) County where resides/ employed/transacts business	OHIO R. CIV. P. 30(B)(5)	OHIO R. CIV. P. 30(C)(2) Objection must be stated concisely in a non-argumentative and non-suggestive manner

State/Territory	Presumptive Number of Depositions	Presumptive Time Limit	Location/Range of Deposition	Rule 30(b)(6) Equivalent	Rules for Defending
Oklahoma	N/A	OKLA. STAT. tit. 12, § 12-3230(A)(3) 6 hours between 8 am and 5 pm (not on Saturday, Sunday or holiday)	OKLA. STAT. tit. 12, § 12-3230(B) Witness in county where resides/adjoining county/ or county of service Party also in county where action pending	OKLA. STAT. tit. 12, § 12-3230(C)(5)	OKLA. STAT. tit. 12, § 12-3230(D) Does not contain limitation of FRCP 30(c) limiting objections to non-argumentative and non-suggestive language
Oregon	N/A	N/A	OR. R. CIV. P. 55(F)(2) Resident in county where resides/employed/ transacts business in person Non-resident in county where served or such other convenient place	OR. R. CIV. P. 39(C)(6)	OR. R. CIV. P. 39(D)(3) Objections stated concisely in non-argumentative and non-suggestive manner

State/Territory	Presumptive Number of Depositions	Presumptive Time Limit	Location/Range of Deposition	Rule 30(b)(6) Equivalent	Rules for Defending
Pennsylvania	N/A	N/A	42 PA. CONS. STAT. § 5905 Any county in state	PA. R. CIV. P. 4007.1(e)	PA. R. CIV. P. 4016 Objections waived if could have been cured at time Does not contain limitation of FRCP 30(c) limiting objections to non-argumentative and non-suggestive language
Rhode Island	N/A	N/A	R.I. SUP. CT. R. CIV. P. 45 No limitations	R.I. SUP. CT. R. CIV. P. 30(b)(6)	R.I. SUP. CT. R. CIV. P. 30(d)(1) Objection stated concisely in non-argumentative and non-suggestive manner R.I. SUP. CT. R. CIV. P. 32(e)(3)(B) Errors that could have been corrected are waived if not raised at time

State/Territory	Presumptive Number of Depositions	Presumptive Time Limit	Location/Range of Deposition	Rule 30(b)(6) Equivalent	Rules for Defending
South Carolina	N/A No depositions in matters less than $10,000 S.C. CIR. R. 87J	N/A	S.C. R. CIV. P. 30(a)(2) County where resides/ employed/transacts business Party also in county where action pending	S.C. R. CIV. P. 30(b)(6)	S.C. R. CIV. P. 30(j) Witness must ask deposing lawyer for clarifications, etc. Counsel shall not make objections that suggest an answer. Objections stated concisely and in non-argumentative and non-suggestive manner, stating basis for objection and nothing more. Counsel and witness may not confer about substance of testimony except for privilege. Deposing lawyer may make inquiries to determine if any coaching occurred and, if so, to what degree

State/Territory	Presumptive Number of Depositions	Presumptive Time Limit	Location/Range of Deposition	Rule 30(b)(6) Equivalent	Rules for Defending
South Dakota	N/A	S.D. CODIFIED LAWS § 15-6-30(d)(2) One 7-hour day	S.D. CODIFIED LAWS § 15-6-45(d)(2) Resident only in county where resides/employed/transacts business/such other convenient place Non-resident only in county where served or such other convenient place	S.D. CODIFIED LAWS § 15-6-30(b)(6)	S.D. CODIFIED LAWS § 15-6-30(d)(1) Objection must be stated concisely and in a non-argumentative and non-suggestive manner
Tennessee	N/A	N/A	TENN. R. CIV. P. 45.04(2) Resident in county where reside/employed/transacts business in person or such other convenient place	TENN. R. CIV. P. 30.02(6)	TENN. R. CIV. P. 30.03 Objection must be stated concisely and in a non-argumentative and non-suggestive manner

State/Territory	Presumptive Number of Depositions	Presumptive Time Limit	Location/Range of Deposition	Rule 30(b)(6) Equivalent	Rules for Defending
Texas	TEX. R. CIV. P. 190.1–190.4 Plaintiff sets level of discovery by cause of action alleged Level 1 has 6 total hours Level 2 has 50 total hours Level 3 determined at pretrial conference	TEX. R. CIV. P. 199.5(c) 6 hours	TEX. R. CIV. P. 199.2(b)(2) Witness in county of residence/employed/ regularly transacts business County of suit for party County of service or within 150 miles for non-resident	TEX. R. CIV. P. 199.2(b)(1)	TEX. R. CIV. P. 199.5(d) Private conferences during the taking of the deposition are improper except to determine privilege. Private conferences allowed during recesses and adjournments. TEX. R. CIV. P. 199.5(e) Objection limited to "objection, form" or "objection, leading" Must give clear and concise reason if requested Argumentative or suggestive objections may be grounds to terminate or for costs or sanctions

State/Territory	Presumptive Number of Depositions	Presumptive Time Limit	Location/Range of Deposition	Rule 30(b)(6) Equivalent	Rules for Defending
Utah	UTAH R. CIV. P. 26(c) creates three tiers based on damages claimed $50,000 or less has 3 total deposition hours Between $50,000 and $300,000 has 15 total hours Over $300,000 has 30 total hours	UTAH R. CIV. P. 30(d) 4 hours for non-party 7 hours for party	UTAH R. CIV. P. 45(c) Resident only in county resides/employed/ transacts business in person Non-resident only in county where served	UTAH R. CIV. P. 30(b)(6)	UTAH R. CIV. P. 30(c)(2) Objections stated concisely and in a non-argumentative and non-suggestive manner
Vermont	N/A	N/A	VT. R. CIV. P. 45(b)(2) May be served anywhere in state VT. R. CIV. P. 45(c)(3)(A) may quash if asks resident to travel more than 50 miles one-way or a non-resident more than 50 miles from place of service	VT. R. CIV. P. 30(b)(6)	VT. R. CIV. P. 30(d)(1) Objection must be stated in non-argumentative and non-suggestive manner

State/Territory	Presumptive Number of Depositions	Presumptive Time Limit	Location/Range of Deposition	Rule 30(b)(6) Equivalent	Rules for Defending
Virginia	N/A	N/A	VA. SUP. CT. R. 4.5(b) Party in county or city where suit pending/ adjacent county or city/ place where parties agree Non-party in county or city where resides/ employed/principal place of business/place where parties agree	VA. SUP. CT. R. 4.5(b)(6)	VA. SUP. CT. R. 4.5(c)(2) Objection must be stated concisely in a non-argumentative and non-suggestive manner
Washington	N/A	N/A	WASH. R. CIV. P. 45(e)(2) Resident only in county where resides/employed/ transacts business Nonresident only in county where served or within 40 miles of service	WASH. R. CIV. P. 30(b)(6)	WASH. R. CIV. P. 30(c) Judge or special master may make telephone rulings on objections during deposition WASH. R. CIV. P. 30(h)(2) Objections shall be concise and shall not suggest or coach answers. Argumentative interruptions are not permitted

State/Territory	Presumptive Number of Depositions	Presumptive Time Limit	Location/Range of Deposition	Rule 30(b)(6) Equivalent	Rules for Defending
West Virginia	N/A	N/A	W. VA. R. CIV. P. 45(c) Deponent only in county where resides/employed/ transacts business	W. VA. R. CIV. P. 30(b)(7)	W. VA. R. CIV. P. 30(d)(1) Objection must be stated concisely and in a non-argumentative and non-suggestive manner
Wisconsin	WIS. R. CIV. P. 804.045 Reasonable number not to exceed 10	WIS. R. CIV. P. 804.045 7 hours	WIS. R. CIV. P. 804.05(3) Party anywhere within 100 miles where party resides/employed/ transacts business Plaintiff also in county where action commenced or pending Non-resident defendant within 100 miles of place of service Resident non-party anywhere within 100 miles where resides/ employed/transacts business/or is served	WIS. R. CIV. P. 804.05(2)(e)	WIS. R. CIV. P. 804.05(4) Does not contain limitation of FRCP 30(c) limiting objections to non-argumentative and non-suggestive language

State/Territory	Presumptive Number of Depositions	Presumptive Time Limit	Location/Range of Deposition	Rule 30(b)(6) Equivalent	Rules for Defending
Wyoming	N/A	WYO. R. CIV. P. 30(d)(1) One 7-hour day	WYO. R. CIV. P. 45(b)(4) Witness only in county where resides/employed/ regularly transacts business Non-resident only in county where served	WYO. R. CIV. P. 30(b)(6)	WYO. R. CIV. P. 30(c) Objection must be stated concisely in a non-argumentative and non-suggestive manner
District of Columbia	D.C. R. CIV. P. 30(a)(2)(A) 10 depositions	D.C. R. CIV. P. 30(d)	D.C. R. CIV. P. 45(a)(1)(A)(iii) Anywhere in district	D.C. R. CIV. P. 30(b)(6)	D.C. R. CIV. P. 30(c)(2) Objection must be stated concisely in a non-argumentative and non-suggestive manner
American Samoa	N/A	N/A	AM. SAM. R. CIV. P. 45 Within Samoa	AM. SAM. R. CIV. P. 30(b)(6)	AM. SAM. R. CIV. P. 30(c)(2) Does not contain limitation of FRCP 30(c) limiting objections to non-argumentative and non-suggestive language

State/Territory	Presumptive Number of Depositions	Presumptive Time Limit	Location/Range of Deposition	Rule 30(b)(6) Equivalent	Rules for Defending
Guam	GUAM R. CIV. P. 30(a)(2)(A) 10 depositions	GUAM R. CIV. P. 30(d)(2) 7 hours	GUAM R. CIV. P. 45 Within Guam	GUAM R. CIV. P. 30(b)(6)	GUAM R. CIV. P. 30(c) Does not contain limitation of FRCP 30(c) limiting objections to non-argumentative and non-suggestive language
Northern Mariana Islands	N. MAR. I. R. CIV. P. 30(a)(2)(A) 10 depositions	N/A	N. MAR. I. R. CIV. P. 30(h)(1) Within the Commonwealth if party resides/has principal place of business at time action commences Outside of the Commonwealth must provide economy round-trip ticket to Commonwealth from residence/place of business	N. MAR. I. R. CIV. P. 30(b)(6)	N. MAR. I. R. CIV. P. 30(d)(1) Objection stated concisely and in a non-argumentative and non-suggestive manner

State/Territory	Presumptive Number of Depositions	Presumptive Time Limit	Location/Range of Deposition	Rule 30(b)(6) Equivalent	Rules for Defending
Puerto Rico	N/A	N/A	P.R. R. PRAC. & PROC. R. 40.4 Resident where resides/employed/transacts business Non-resident only where served	P.R. R. PRAC. & PROC. R. 27.5	P.R. R. PRAC. & PROC. R. 27.5 Does not contain limitation of FRCP 30(c) limiting objections to non-argumentative and non-suggestive language
U.S. Virgin Islands	Adopts Federal Rules	Adopts Federal Rules	No specific rule	Adopts Federal Rules	V.I. SUP. CT. R. 39(b) Counsel shall refrain from any conduct that impedes, delays, or otherwise frustrates fair and reasonable examination, including: (i) coaching through objections other than stating objection with brief description of basis; (ii) directing

State/Territory	Presumptive Number of Depositions	Presumptive Time Limit	Location/Range of Deposition	Rule 30(b)(6) Equivalent	Rules for Defending
U.S. Virgin Islands *(cont'd)*					not to answer unless privileged; (iii) leading witness with respect to times, dates, documents, testimony, etc.

Index

(References are to question numbers, unless otherwise indicated.)

A

C

D

E

F

N

O

P

Q

S